ON DESTINY

ON DESTINY

A Philosophical Dialogue

Nicholas J. Pappas

Algora Publishing
New York

Library of Congress Cataloging-in-Publication Data —

Names: Pappas, Nicholas J., author.
Title: On destiny: a philosophical dialogue / Nicholas J. Pappas.
Description: New York: Algora Publishing, 2016.
Identifiers: LCCN 2016040805 (print) | LCCN 2016041371 (ebook) | ISBN
    9781628942286 (soft cover: alk. paper) | ISBN 9781628942293 (hard cover:
    alk. paper) | ISBN 9781628942309 (pdf)
Subjects: LCSH: Fate and fatalism.
Classification: LCC BJ1461 .P34 2016 (print) | LCC BJ1461 (ebook) | DDC
    123—dc23
LC record available at https://lccn.loc.gov/2016040805

Printed in the United States

TABLE OF CONTENTS

INTRODUCTION

Dear Reader,

Have you ever wondered about your destiny? Or maybe you're one who wonders why others wonder about their destiny. In either case, this is a book for you.

This book is a dialogue. That means it's not a treatise with a clearly spelled out central thesis or grand conclusion that I can summarize here. It's more of a philosophical play, meant to be enjoyed, and meant to challenge the reader to conclude on her or his own what it all means.

The main character, Director, plays the role of philosopher. What is a philosopher? The standard answer is that a philosopher is a lover of wisdom. But there is always more to any given philosopher.

In Director's case, he does as his name suggests. He manages to lead, or at least influence, the direction and shape of the dialogue. He gives it its philosophical tone.

The other characters — Friend, Scientist, and Artist — all have their own notions of destiny. Director tries to tease out the full meaning of their ideas.

Friend opens the book by noting that destiny seems more hopeful, promising, than the ancient notion of fate. At the end, he says every fulfilled destiny serves as inspiration to others. A seed produces a flower, which produces more seeds. This brings a sort of immortality.

Director questions this: "But what guarantee is there that the cycle will go on?" Friend replies: "There's nothing inevitable when it comes to human things."

If true, this means there's much at stake. Everything is at stake. The book ends with these lines:

"Director: That's a lot of pressure on people of destiny, no?

"Friend: True, but they're used to pressure from simply living their lives.

"Director: Then there's no need to train them for greater affairs?

"Friend: No, there isn't. They're part of the greater in just being them-selves."

And that sums it up nicely. But now it may seem I've given some sort of final statement when I said there was none.

By way of apology, I'll note that an ending never makes full sense with-out knowing the beginning and middle. What does Scientist have to say about all this? What does Artist believe? I'll leave that to you.

Artist and Scientist are individual characters, but they, to a significant degree, represent their types. Does Friend represent the type 'friend'? I think that's a harder question than it might seem. Do all friends share something in common with Friend? Perhaps the better question is: Do all of Director's friends?

So here I offer one of the keys to the book. The reader must answer: What do Artist, Scientist, and Friend have in common? And what do they have in common with Director? But, and perhaps more importantly: How do they differ from him?

Sorry if that seems more riddle than key. But sometimes the key is to know all the riddles.

I hope you enjoy the book.

Nick Pappas

Fate (Friend)

Friend: What did the ancient Greeks think about fate?

Director: They believed in three immortals who determined it.

Friend: Why three and not just one?

Director: Each performed a different function. One spun fate's thread, one measured its length, and one made the cut.

Friend: And this power of theirs stretched over all mortals?

Director: Yes, and some say over the gods, too.

Friend: Then these Fates must often have been cruel.

Director: Why do you say that?

Friend: Because life is often cruel. Do you think the Fates enjoyed their cruelty?

Director: I suspect they did, or at least it didn't bother them much.

Friend: Well, then they weren't worth believing in, were they?

Director: I don't think they were.

Friend: But do you know what is worth believing in?

Director: No, tell me.

Friend: Destiny.

Director: What's the difference between destiny and fate?

Friend: Destiny seems more promising, more hopeful than fate.

Director: Can you say why?

Friend: It's just a feeling I have. And I know I'm not alone in this. But don't you agree?

Director: With how destiny seems? I'm inclined to agree.

Friend: I'm glad, Director. Because we all need something to believe in — other than cruel old fate.

DESTINY (ARTIST)

Artist: A goddess called Destiny? Ha! Well, Director, I suppose there would be benefits to that.

Director: Such as?

Artist: For one, a goddess can have singleness of purpose.

Director: You don't think the Fates worked well together?

Artist: How can we possibly know if they did or if they didn't?

Director: But what about Destiny? What do we know about her singleness of purpose? What if sometimes she feels like this, and sometimes she feels like that?

Artist: But who would you rather try to understand? Three changeable beings or one?

Director: Fair enough, assuming the Fates ever changed. But what do we try to understand?

Artist: The way that Destiny governs our lives.

Director: But if she sometimes feels like this and sometimes feels like that....

Artist: Yes, yes. But Destiny will give us signs of her current intent.

Director: And do we need to pray to her to know the meanings of these signs?

Artist: Of course not. People must learn to construe the signs themselves.

Director: But what comes of learning what the signs all mean? Won't our destiny be the same regardless of what we know?

Artist: As the signs change so too do the choices we can make.

Director: So Destiny offers choices to those who know the signs, and that's how she rules our lives?

Artist: Yes. But through it all there's always one basic choice to make.

Director: Oh?

Artist: Stand with her — or simply accept your fate.

The Future (Scientist)

Scientist: Is there a way to know someone's destiny? Scientifically? Of course not.

Director: But if there were, is that something science would want to know?

Scientist: We're not talking about astrology? We're talking about real knowledge?

Director: Yes.

Scientist: How would science even begin to come to a knowledge of the future like that?

Director: I suppose it could perfect the sciences of genetics, sociology, political science, psychology, and so on.

Scientist: But no science is ever perfect. There's always more to know.

Director: However true that may be, Scientist, what if these sciences came to know enough?

Scientist: Enough to know someone's destiny? Ridiculous.

Director: But if science masters nature, nurture, and choice — which is essentially what the sciences I mentioned are about — won't it know enough to piece together the future in broad strokes? Or don't you think science can ever come to master these things?

Scientist: Nature? Yes. Nurture? Possibly. Choice? Never.

Director: Not even if we narrow the available choices?

Scientist: Limit the choices we can make in order to make prediction easier?

Director: Well?

Scientist: Who would agree to that?

Director: People who like predictability.

Scientist: Even if this were possible, it's a long way off.

Director: But do you think it's a worthwhile goal, to know these things?

Scientist: Not at the cost of freedom.

Director: Then I trust you'll do your best to ensure we never pay that price.

Belief (Friend)

Friend: What I want to know is if you believe in yourself strongly enough, will you necessarily achieve your destiny?

Director: Well, that supposes you know who you are. Otherwise you might believe in someone you dreamed up. No?

Friend: True.

Director: So the first step is knowledge. But that's a funny thing. Because if you have knowledge you don't need belief.

Friend: What do you mean?

Director: Look at it this way. If I think about whether you're paying attention, I can do one of two things. I can believe you're paying attention, or you're not. Or I can know you're paying attention, or you're not. If I know you're paying attention, do I have any need to believe you're paying attention? Do you know what I'm asking?

Friend: I know. And the answer is no, there's no need to believe.

Director: Similarly, if I know who I am, do I have to believe in who I am?

Friend: No. But don't you have to believe in yourself in the sense that you believe you'll live out your destiny and prevail in the end?

Director: That seems to me to be a different kind of belief, Friend, a belief that has to do with probabilities.

Friend: You mean the odds that we'll come out on top?

Director: Yes. And we need to be honest here. If the odds seem bad, very bad...

Friend: ...we find a better fight to fight.

Director: But does that mean we abandon our destiny?

Friend: No, of course not. We simply choose our battles, as they say.

Director: And since we can never know with certainty if we'll win?

Friend: Then, Director, I think it never hurts to allow ourselves to believe — just a little in our luck.

BAD AND GOOD (ARTIST)

Artist: If you don't believe in your destiny you won't achieve your destiny. But then again, that might be best.

Director: How so?

Artist: What if your destiny is bad? Or do you think all destinies are good?

Director: No, some destinies are bad.

Artist: Well, what if you live up to a bad destiny? Success?

Director: You're very clever, Artist.

Artist: Ha! Well, thank you. But what's the answer? Shall we say it's a failure?

Director: Let's.

Artist: Good. Now what about the other way?

Director: You mean when you don't live up to your bad destiny?

Artist: Yes. Is that a success?

Director: I'm more inclined to say it's neutral.

Artist: Is there a way to go from neutral to good?

Director: If there is it's up to the goddess. So let's hope she gives the neutrals a sign.

Artist: Agreed. Now let's sum things up.

Director: Alright. First there's success: living up to your good destiny. Then there's the neutral: failing to live up to your bad destiny. Finally we have the failures: failing to live up to your good destiny, and living up to your bad destiny. But there's something I'm wondering.

Artist: Oh? What's that?

Director: You said, basically, if you don't believe you won't live up to your belief. So why can't we help people with bad destinies to just not believe?

Artist: Yes, yes. But it's easy to believe in the bad. And when it's easy to believe — it's hard to let go.

Unbelief (Scientist)

Scientist: Oh, Director, I have real doubts that destiny exists in any meaningful form.

Director: Not even in the sense that you're destined to be a great scientist?

Scientist: Spare me the flattery. We work for what we achieve. And what we achieve is our destiny. It's not some given written in the stars.

Director: When did you decide to become a scientist?

Scientist: When I was a little boy.

Director: How did you decide?

Scientist: Science always fascinated me.

Director: So you followed your fascination.

Scientist: Yes.

Director: Can't we say it's our destiny to follow what fascinates us?

Scientist: But why do we need to introduce destiny? Why can't we just say we follow what fascinates us and that's all there is to it?

Director: I see no harm in that.

Scientist: Good. Because sometimes it seems the idea of destiny is to take credit away from where credit is due. Do you know what I mean? It wasn't my struggles that brought me success. It was all destined to be.

Director: I know what you mean.

Scientist: And then people ask, Why were you chosen while others weren't? And I tell them, We all were chosen — but some of us do something with ourselves while others don't.

Director: And how do they react to that?

Scientist: They say I'm insensitive.

Director: Are they right?

Scientist: Some people are very sensitive to truth. So I think I'll just leave it at that.

NATIONS (FRIEND)

Friend: Nations all have the same fate.

Director: What makes you say that?

Friend: They all rise and fall.

Director: But there's a lot that can happen in the rising and the falling, don't you think?

Friend: True.

Director: And I'm not even sure all nations must rise and then fall.

Friend: What do you mean?

Director: Can't they plateau and stay that way a long, long time?

Friend: And then they might further rise?

Director: Or fall a bit, too. Yes. And then they might rise. And fall. And so on, and so on.

Friend: So it's not as simple as a nation rises and then it falls?

Director: No, I don't think it is.

Friend: But all nations do eventually come to an end, don't they?

Director: I'm not sure that's necessarily true.

Friend: A nation could last forever?

Directory: It's possible, don't you think?

Friend: Well, how could we bring this about?

Director: First and foremost, I think it would take a great deal of luck.

Friend: I agree. What else?

Director: Then it would take great and wise leaders.

Friend: Is there anything else?

Director: Yes. The citizens would have to have reason to believe in the cause. So there's luck, leadership, and belief. And that, my friend, is what destines a nation to last.

Epic (Artist)

Artist: I prefer to tell epic tales.

Director: And what makes a tale epic?

Artist: Oh, you know, Director. Heroic deeds and adventures over an extended period of time.

Director: Does the backdrop matter much? I'm always curious about backdrops.

Artist: Of course it matters. If it's used well, it helps bring the individuals of the work into high relief.

Director: When you bring your characters into relief, do you wish you were like them?

Artist: Wish I were made to stand out? No, I leave that to my characters. I'm content to blend into the background. But what about you? You'd make a good character in one of my tales.

Director: Oh? Why?

Artist: Because you're not sure whether you want to stand out.

Director: Why do you think that?

Artist: Because you come close but then never thrust yourself forward.

Director: Maybe I'm meant to be like you and to never stand out.

Artist: No, I never find you in the background with me.

Director: Where am I then?

Artist: You're consistently in the middle, the middle ground, my friend.

Director: So why would I make a good character?

Artist: Because there's great drama in moving from middle to front.

Director: But what if the middle is my front?

Artist: 'Front' as in a war? Ha! Then I would love to see more of what you do in your epic middle ground fight.

SCIENCE AND TECHNOLOGY (SCIENTIST)

Scientist: Of all the sciences you mentioned I think political science is the one most questionable.

Director: Why?

Scientist: Because it's not at all clear to me whether it's a true science or a pseudo science.

Director: Is that because it sometimes meddles with the future?

Scientist: Yes. It likes to predict what will happen.

Director: Does it go beyond that? Does it think it's destined to help shape the future?

Scientist: I think it sometimes does.

Director: And you don't think that's the proper role of science?

Scientist: Science wants to know, not shape.

Director: But technology, the child of science, seeks to shape. Doesn't it?

Scientist: True. But I've never really told you what I think of technology.

Director: Well?

Scientist: Technology and this sort of political science are of a piece.

Director: Both shaping without knowing in the scientific sense?

Science: Yes.

Director: But what better way to know than to shape?

Science: To know what can be done, yes. But not to know what is — or even what will be.

Director: But, Scientist, don't you need to know what is before you can know what can be done?

Science: No, Director, you can know what can be done and then proceed to trample all that is.

History (Friend)

Friend: A man of destiny once said: 'The further backward you can look, the further forward you are likely to see.'

Director: Well, a man of destiny should know. But do you think what he says about looking into the future mists is true?

Friend: I don't know. I mean how do we really see into the past?

Director: We should ask a historian.

Friend: Sure. But they often think they can see more than they actually see.

Director: But how would you know that? I mean, wouldn't you have to be able to see into the past in order to judge?

Friend: No. You can see when unanswered questions exist. And if the historians think they've answered the unanswered — you know.

Director: So the best historians know what they don't know. But what are histories about, at bottom?

Friend: Two things. Nations and individuals. And you can't write about one without the other.

Director: But what about biographies that don't talk about the nation?

Friend: The nation is the backdrop to the life, Director. It's there even if you don't want it to be.

Director: So the destiny of all individuals is tied up with the destiny of the nation. But is the destiny of the nation tied up with the destiny of all its individuals?

Friend: That's a funny question to ask.

Director: Why?

Friend: Because the individuals are subsumed into 'the people'. And the destiny of the nation is, of course, tied up with them.

Director: But sometimes the people are divided into parts.

Friends: Yes, and how those parts strive to make their whole is what history is all about.

The Past (Artist)

Artist: There's an art to telling and remembering the past. It's not a science.

Director: What would make it a science?

Artist: What makes anything a science?

Director: I suppose you have to have observation and experimentation.

Artist: Well, there's so much of the past that we can never observe. And what would it mean to experiment on things gone by?

Director: So what's the art?

Artist: I'll let you in on the trick. The telling shapes the remembering.

Director: That's an awful trick.

Artist: But it's the only game in town!

Director: Even at the personal level?

Artist: At every level.

Director: So to the extent our destiny is rooted in our past, do you really think we can shape that destiny by lying to ourselves about our past?

Artist: Yes.

Director: But how much shaping does the past admit?

Artist: As much as we're willing to believe.

Director: Then what can we do to keep from believing these things?

Artist: Know the truth.

Director: How do we know the truth about the past?

Artist: You don't know? Ha! We have to have seen it ourselves with our own two eyes. And even then....

Director: And even then what?

Artist: We might not understand what we saw.

THE PAST (SCIENTIST)

Scientist: A truly scientific account of the past, at least our near past, may one day be possible.

Director: How so?

Scientist: Think of it like this, by way of metaphor. When we observe the light from far off stars, we're seeing the past.

Director: That's our current understanding, yes.

Scientist: Well, imagine if we had such light for things much, much closer to home.

Director: I think I know what you're getting at, Scientist. But even if we find a way to see such light, to what extent should we?

Scientist: To the furthest extent possible.

Director: Even if that light could reveal our own past thoughts?

Scientist: What a wonderful thing that would be!

Director: Why?

Scientist: Wouldn't you like to know what great leaders, great poets, great philosophers were thinking?

Director: Hmm. But what about our neighbors?

Scientist: What about them?

Director: Are we destined to know what they were thinking, too?

Scientist: Yes, I know what you mean. I suppose we'd limit our use of the light.

Director: Yes, that's probably wise. But how would we decide?

Scientist: Decide on when to use it? Why not start with volunteers?

Director: Those who would be willing to, quite literally, bare their souls? But what kind of person would do that?

Scientist: Oh, you might be surprised.

Forgetting (Friend)

Friend: Some things are too good, too important to forget.

Director: But what if we do forget?

Friend: The point is that we can't forget, even if we wanted to.

Director: Why do you think that is?

Friend: Because the memories shape us.

Director: They actively shape us?

Friend: Yes, of course.

Director: So they truly are living memories?

Friend: That's a good way of putting it.

Director: To lose them would be, in a sense, to die?

Friend: Yes.

Director: And even if we don't die, at the least we'd be lost, cast adrift?

Friend: We would.

Director: But with these living memories, where are we?

Friend: Living as we should.

Director: And what does our future bring?

Friend: Who can say what the future will bring?

Director: But whatever it is, is it our destiny?

Friend: It is.

Director: Because our living memories shape us toward our destined end?

Friend: Exactly.

Director: And the only way not to live that destiny is to forget, to cut ourselves free?

Friend: Yes. But I'm not sure I'd call that 'free'.

Laws (Artist)

Artist: You can't create meaningful art without taking certain things as given.

Director: Given? In what sense?

Artist: Immutable.

Director: Would you extend what you're saying? Can you have a meaningful life without taking certain things as given?

Artist: Oh, I don't know. Why do you ask me such questions?

Director: Because I think you might know. But why do you say you don't?

Artist: Because art and life differ. The something you create in art is always based on something firm.

Director: And that's not how it is with life?

Artist: Of course it's not. We very often try to build on mush.

Director: But can't your art portray someone who builds on mushy ground?

Artist: Yes, yes — of course. But in art there's always something firm beyond whatever might be soft.

Director: A sort of law of nature of the work?

Artist: Yes. Good art will always have its given laws.

Director: Laws given by the artist?

Artist: Right. And each work has its own characteristic set.

Director: Then I really can't see why you don't say life is like art.

Artist: Why can't you see why? Because we all have characteristic laws, personal laws so to speak? I don't believe that's true.

Director: But even if only some of us do, do you think good personal laws correspond to good taste in art?

Artist: I do. And to good destiny, too.

CHAOS (SCIENTIST)

Scientist: Certainly there are givens. There would be no science without the given.

Director: In other words, everything can't be a variable?

Scientist: Yes. Then you have chaos.

Director: Isn't it the same with destiny?

Scientist: Ah, destiny again. How so?

Director: A wide open destiny isn't destiny. It's chaos. Does that make sense?

Scientist: Yes, I think it does. But how do you know what's given in your destiny?

Director: How do we know what we can change in our lives and what we can't? I don't know that there's an easy answer to that question, Scientist.

Scientist: Then we must try, experiment. See what our true limitations are.

Director: And what if instead of proper limits we find none?

Scientist: Oh, that's the myth of unlimited potential. There are always limits.

Director: And if always limits then never chaos?

Scientist: Not true chaos. All seeming chaos is just that because we have yet to discover the limits, the order in it.

Director: But what if an element of chaos is a given in the core of our being?

Scientist: A mysterious life force or something like that?

Director: Sure. What if that beautiful force is what gives shape to our destiny?

Scientist: I suppose it's possible. But I'd like to learn the laws of this seemingly chaotic thing.

Director: In order to tame it?

Scientist: No, Director. Just because you understand a thing that doesn't make it tame.

Director: But what would we do with our understanding of this force?

Scientist: Find the right food to nourish it — and see if we don't thrive.

Chaos (Friend)

Friend: Chaos? True chaos? There's no such thing.

Director: You believe there's always some sort of order?

Friend: At bottom? Yes.

Director: But there's order and then there's order. So what would you say to those who emphatically claim their destiny is chaotic, if not perfectly so?

Friend: I'd ask them what kind of destiny that is.

Director: What if they say it's one of great freedom?

Friend: No, I don't think they'd say that. But even if they did, I'd tell them that to the extent there's chaos, they aren't truly free. They have no control over their lives. And isn't lack of control exactly what makes you a slave?

Director: But who really has control over life?

Friend: Yes, but there's control and then there's control. And if no one has control, are we saying no one has a free life?

Director: Well, are we sure control over our lives is what makes us free?

Friend: Absolutely sure.

Director: And there's no control where there's chaos?

Friend: Right.

Director: What's the opposite of chaos?

Friend: Order, as you said.

Director: Does order help keep us free?

Friend: Yes, of course.

Director: But don't certain kinds of order, bad order, make us the opposite of free?

Friend: Sure. They oppress.

Director: Then, in those cases, couldn't a dash of disorder give us a taste of being free?

Order (Artist)

Artist: Destiny respects no order of things. Destiny is a great destroyer.

Director: What gives it this awesome power?

Artist: Why, the human beings whose lives it shapes.

Director: But could this mean that destiny is more concerned with the powerful than the weak?

Artist: Of course! Did you ever have any doubt?

Director: I did, actually. But tell me. What if the weak band together?

Artist: Then they, as a whole, are of interest to the destroyer.

Director: Alright. But what does destiny want to destroy?

Artist: What else? The order of things.

Director: In order to create a new order of things?

Artist: Doesn't a new order necessarily follow once the old order is gone?

Director: I suppose that's true. But here's a problem I can't seem to get around.

Artist: What problem?

Director: You're saying some will be destined to destroy the old order.

Artist: I am.

Director: Then doesn't it follow that some will be destined to protect that order?

Artist: Of course.

Director: But then destiny for them won't be a destroyer. Do you see what I mean?

Artist: Yes, yes. But it's their destiny to be destroyed by the very destiny they live!

Director: Assuming the old order is destroyed.

Artist: The old order is always destroyed, eventually. And I can see how you might be confused. The destroyers often give the new order the old order's name. And what destroys so thoroughly as that?

Order (Scientist)

Scientist: To the extent we learn the laws of destiny? We'd have found our eternal order.

Director: And how would we set to learning these laws?

Scientist: We'd bring all of the sciences to bear on the individual.

Director: In order to see what he or she will be?

Scientist: Yes. Given such and such a genetic makeup, and such and such an upbringing, and so on — this is what you'll be. But that seems impossible, no?

Director: It certainly seems that way at times. But I thought science was more interested in the what-is rather than the what-will-be.

Scientist: Science is interested in it all — the past, the present, and the future, too.

Director: Hmm. But let's stay with the future for now. Doesn't an interest in what someone will be assume one great constant?

Scientist: What have you got in mind?

Director: The world. The world would have to stay the same in order to know what someone's destiny will be. Or don't you think the world affects our destinies?

Scientist: Of course it does. And that's where the second half of the effort comes in.

Director: The second half?

Scientist: Yes. Actively forecasting on an ongoing basis what the world will be.

Director: Like some sort of long range weather report? A certain sort of person, under a certain sort of 'weather', will end up a certain way?

Scientist: Yes, speaking more or less broadly and allowing for choice.

Director: But doesn't choice ruin everything, ruin the quest for order?

Scientist: I've given this some thought, and I hate to say it — but not necessarily. We could factor in a range of all possible choices and still be able to predict.

Director: And that would be that. But really, Scientist, all of this is truly impossible, no?

Scientist: I'm starting to have my doubts.

Humanity (Friend)

Friend: Does humanity have a fixed destiny or do we shape it ourselves?

Director: I don't know, Friend.

Friend: Assuming we shape it, what do you think that means?

Director: Maybe it means we fight against the fixed and absolute — and win.

Friend: Do you think that holds for individuals, too? I mean, what if you don't shape your destiny?

Director: I guess we'd say you failed.

Friend: I think this is important. Can you say more?

Director: Well, look at it this way. Imagine your destiny to be like a lump of clay. Some lumps are big. Some are small. Some are hard. Some are soft. And so on. But each is a thing that can be shaped. Is it enough to say at the end of your life, I kept my lump intact?

Friend: No, I think if it can be shaped, it ought to be shaped — into a beautiful thing. Don't you?

Director: Yes. Now, how does this apply to humanity as a whole?

Friend: I suppose it means humanity has its clay. And we all give it shape.

Director: But do we give it shape? I mean, how can we as mere individuals shape humanity's destiny?

Friend: By shaping our own.

Director: We trust that our own destiny will somehow help humanity take care of itself?

Friend: Yes. After all, isn't humanity really just the sum of its parts?

Director: Maybe. And then again it might be something more, or less. But what would you say to those who aren't content to be mere parts?

Friend: They want to give shape to, or even be, humanity itself? I don't know.

Director: You don't know because you're so impressed by their boldness you're left without speech? Or is it because, as I suspect, you're thinking something else?

Failure (Artist)

Artist: So many artists are destined to fail. Why shouldn't humanity as a whole be destined that way, too?

Director: Does it matter to you if the other artists fail so long as you succeed?

Artist: Not in the least.

Director: But it matters to you if humanity itself fails?

Artist: And I succeed? No, why should it?

Director: Well, you're refreshingly honest if nothing else, my friend.

Artist: The trick is not to tether yourself to anyone else's success.

Director: You stand on your own.

Artist: Yes.

Director: Now, when you stand on your own as concerns other artists — what are you?

Artist: Someone who might have the makings of a great artist.

Director: And when you stand on your own as concerns humanity?

Artist: Well....

Director: Well?

Artist: You want me to say I'm inhuman, a monster.

Director: Are you?

Artist: Alright, alright. I stand with humanity. But if it fails it won't be my fault.

Director: Why not?

Artist: Why not? Because I only make art! I don't lead anyone down dangerous paths.

Director: Then who leads us down the dangerous paths?

Artist: Blame the politicians, leaders, or statesmen — whatever you call them.

Director: But who inspires them to be what they are? Could it be... you?

Success (Scientist)

Scientist: Is science destined to succeed? If people live up to it, then yes.

Director: What does it take to live up to science?

Scientist: I think you'll think I'm crazy if I tell you.

Director: Oh, I don't know about that.

Scientist: Alright. I'll tell you. It takes cleanliness.

Director: Cleanliness?

Scientist: See? I told you.

Director: Are you talking about mental cleanliness?

Scientist: Yes, but also general cleanliness.

Director: Because science is neat and orderly?

Scientist: At its best, yes. Oh, and I know we study some very messy things. But even if we're studying chaos we go about it in an orderly way.

Director: Tell me about mental cleanliness.

Scientist: It means to be clear in your thinking.

Director: Even when studying something murky?

Scientist: Especially when studying something murky.

Director: And the more people who are clear, the greater the success of science?

Scientist: Absolutely.

Director: But what if they're clear and yet they're wrong? Is that possible?

Scientist: Yes, it happens from time to time. But it should be easy to correct.

Director: I don't know, Scientist. Don't these people believe they walk with science?

Scientist: Yes, that's true.

Director: Then with that kind of support — why would they listen to you?

IMPACT (FRIEND)

Friend: Are certain people destined to meet? If a certain person changes your life, it sure seems like destiny.

Director: Changes your life for better or for worse?

Friend: Either or both.

Director: Both? How can someone change your life for both better and worse?

Friend: Suppose I meet a woman who lights up my life. But then she's gone. My world seems darker than before.

Director: Hmm. I don't know about that example, Friend. But tell me this. Can't we say we're destined to meet everyone we meet? That everyone changes our life in a sense? Do you know what I'm asking?

Friend: Yes, I know. It's true in a sense, as you say.

Director: But you don't think it's simply true.

Friend: No, I don't. Those we're truly destined to meet make a big impact on our lives.

Director: Suppose you meet someone who makes little impact on you. But you make a great impact on them. Is it destiny for them but not for you?

Friend: Well, I don't like to say that. It seems sort of... conceited.

Director: So how can we say it's destiny for both?

Friend: We can say that whenever you influence someone greatly it always comes back around to you. A sort of karma, if you know what I mean.

Director: So impact on others brings impact on you, inevitably?

Friend: Yes.

Director: And good impact brings good impact, and bad impact bad?

Friend: Don't you think that's how it works? I mean it's karma, right?

Director: But what if the impact is both good and bad?

Friend: Then maybe it cancels itself — and it's almost as if it had never happened at all.

Bias (Artist)

Artist: Artists are biased toward destiny.

Director: How so?

Artist: In good art everything has a purpose. Yes?

Director: Yes.

Artist: Well, if everything has a purpose then every 'chance event' comes to be part of a character's destiny.

Director: What would it take for artists to lose their bias?

Artist: They'd have to deal in random and meaningless events.

Director: That doesn't sound very interesting.

Artist: It depends on what those events are.

Director: Now what about people in real life? Are they biased toward destiny?

Artist: You know some of them are.

Director: And is it as with the artists? They can lose their bias by seeing the events in their lives as meaningless and random?

Artist: Yes, it's the same as with artists.

Director: Are the people who lose their bias happy?

Artist: Some are. Some aren't.

Director: What about you, Artist? Would you be happy with a random, meaningless life?

Artist: If it's a pleasant life? Sure. Why not? What about you?

Director: I'd side with the artists who are partial toward destiny.

Artist: Because you think your life isn't random? Because you think it has meaning?

Director: As for randomness? I leave it to the gods. And as for meaning?

Artist: Let me guess. It's up to you.

Destinies (Scientist)

Scientist: Have I come around to believing I have a destiny? I'm more inclined to believe that science has a destiny and I play a humble part.

Director: Do you think many people see themselves as part of a greater destiny?

Scientist: I think so.

Director: What are some of those destinies?

Scientist: Well, for one it could be a person's nation — especially in times of stress.

Director: What else?

Scientist: I think globalization has brought several greater destinies into play.

Director: Such as?

Scientist: Democracy, human rights, free trade.

Director: Are there any other greater destinies out there?

Scientist: Sure, family can be destiny. Religions. Schools. There are many.

Director: So tell me, Scientist. What about those who don't see themselves as part of a greater destiny?

Scientist: I suppose there are two types. Those who don't see themselves as having a destiny. And those who do.

Director: Do you think there's anything wrong with seeing yourself without a destiny?

Scientist: No, I don't.

Director: And what if you see yourself with a destiny but don't want to be part of anything greater than yourself?

Scientist: I think that's fine — so long as your destiny doesn't interfere with the greater destinies.

Director: The greater destinies take precedence over your individual destiny? Why?

Scientist: For the age old reason that the good of the many outweighs the good of the one. That, and if you interfere with them, they'll interfere with you.

Help (Friend)

Friend: If I knew, just knew I had a destiny? I'd keep it to myself.

Director: Why?

Friend: Because it's nobody's business but mine.

Director: But what if you need people to help you with your destiny?

Friend: I should be able to do it on my own.

Director: Tell me. Do you think I have a destiny?

Friend: I do.

Director: Do you think I do it on my own?

Friend: Of course I do.

Director: Well, my friend, you're mistaken.

Friend: Who helps you?

Director: My friends.

Friend: I help you?

Director: Yes, of course.

Friend: But how can I be helping if I'm not even aware I'm helping?

Director: Sometimes that's the best kind of help.

Friend: Then I want you to help me like that.

Director: What if I've been helping you all along without knowing it?

Friend: I don't see how that can be. I don't even know what my destiny is!

Director: Then maybe I'm helping you prepare the ground.

Friend: Yes, Director, but now you're coming dangerously close to being aware of your help!

Director: Then quick! I'd better stand back — and hope I can help in ways I can't see.

WORKS (ARTIST)

Artist: Of course I believe works of art have a life of their own. And that means they have their own destiny, too.

Director: A destiny separate than that of the artist?

Artist: Yes. Think of it like this. A child has a destiny independent from that of its mother and father. No?

Director: Yes. But it seems different with artists and their work.

Artist: How?

Director: If a work of art achieves fame, the artist, too, achieves fame.

Artist: Not if the work was done anonymously.

Director: Fair enough. But if it wasn't?

Artist: Then the artist is famous.

Director: And it's the same with influence? If the work of art is influential, the artist, too, is influential?

Artist: Yes, it's the same. But art transcends. An artist can have the worst possible personal destiny, but the work of art generally remains unaffected.

Director: It has an independent destiny.

Artist: Right. And that's the point.

Director: But I'm not sure I understand why this seems so important to you.

Artist: It's simple. I'm not worthy of my art.

Director: But how can that be? Of course you're worthy. You created it.

Artist: I'm just a medium through which great art passes.

Director: That may be. But the art chose to pass through you. Why do you think that is? I mean, why not pass through me?

Artist: It chooses me because I accept exactly what's sent. You, my friend, wouldn't accept until you'd asked a thousand questions first. And even then....

Symbiosis (Scientist)

Scientist: Do I believe scientific discoveries have a life of their own? No.

Director: Why not?

Scientist: Because discoveries mean nothing unless people make use of them.

Director: I suppose you'd say the same about science.

Scientist: Science is a bit different. It's much greater than any individual discovery.

Director: Great enough to have a life of its own?

Scientist: I don't know. I mean, does science exist without scientists?

Director: Do scientists exist without science?

Scientist: You have a point.

Director: So let's say they exist together.

Scientist: Yes, let's. But now you're making me think, Director. Science may well have a life of its own.

Director: What does it mean for science to have its own life? Could it mean it has its own destiny?

Scientist: Let's say that's true.

Director: Alright. And if it has its own destiny, does it go its own way?

Scientist: I think we should say yes — provided we allow it to go its own way.

Director: If it goes its own way, do scientists follow or lead?

Scientist: I think we have to say scientists follow wherever science leads.

Director: You're sure scientists don't lead and science follows?

Scientist: Well, we could say that in a sense. After all, the more scientists discover the more we might say that science lives. But the more that science lives the more scientists do, too. I mean, aren't we most alive when doing what we do best? So I think there's symbiosis here — and at best, there are two destinies always on the verge of becoming one.

WORKS AND DISCOVERIES (FRIEND)

Friend: I guess I have to say I prefer artistic works to scientific discoveries.

Director: Why?

Friend: They're more alive.

Director: How so?

Friend: Art speaks to me in a way that science doesn't.

Director: But don't you think there are those to whom science speaks more than art?

Friend: But can you really compare a great book, a great piece of music, a great painting — to something someone comes up with in a lab?

Director: Of course you can. Tell me, what does a great work of art do?

Friend: It enriches our lives.

Director: Can't a great scientific discovery do the same?

Friend: Well, yes. But it's one thing to learn how to build a better widget and it's another thing to stimulate your mind.

Director: Ah, you're saying something interesting.

Friend: What am I saying?

Director: That there's a difference between the end products of science and those of art.

Friend: Of course there is. But what do you think that difference is?

Director: The end product of art, art itself, if it's good, always stimulates the mind. Right?

Friend: Certainly — as long as a person is willing to take it in.

Director: Yes. But the end product of science? It's two things, no? The knowledge itself and the technology that comes of it. Or wouldn't you say technology comes of science?

Friend: Of course I would. But technology doesn't necessarily make you think. So people can enjoy the fruits of science without any thought. But they must think to appreciate the fruits of good art. And so, in my view, art is destined to be superior to science in this very way.

CHARACTERS (ARTIST)

Artist: Characters who believe they have a destiny are more interesting to more people than those who don't.

Director: Why?

Artist: People like to cheer for them.

Director: Would they ever cheer for those who believe they don't have a destiny?

Artist: Sure — if the author makes it clear there's a destiny the character just doesn't know about yet.

Director: It sounds like people are cheering for the destiny more than the character.

Artist: I think there's some truth to that.

Director: Why would they do that? Is destiny that important?

Artist: People see it as giving meaning to life.

Director: You can't have meaning without destiny?

Artist: Of course you can. I'm just telling you what people think.

Director: So how would you get people interested in a character who has no destiny? But maybe you should first tell me what it means to have no destiny.

Artist: Ha! You won't like what I have to say. To have no destiny means to be free.

Director: Interesting. I suppose the audience won't like that definition.

Artist: No, they'll hate it.

Director: So if you portray characters who are 'free' they'll hate them, too?

Artist: The audience, for the most part, believes everyone has a destiny — at least major characters. So a major character free of destiny is pretty much inconceivable to them.

Director: Then all good art has major characters with destinies?

Artist: If 'good' means 'popular', then the answer is usually yes. And now I'll answer your earlier question. The only way to get most people interested in a character with no destiny is to make that character an object of pity. But that distorts the truth.

Hypotheses (Scientist)

Scientist: I always cheer for those who make bold hypotheses.

Director: Why?

Scientist: Oh, because it's exciting!

Director: But aren't most of these hypotheses destined to be wrong?

Scientist: Yes, of course. But when they're right? It's wonderful.

Director: But what about the safe bets? Wouldn't you say it's wonderful when they turn out right?

Scientist: Well, yes, of course I would. Science needs the steady progress that comes from conservative hypotheses.

Director: So not everyone can make the big bets?

Scientist: No, not everyone can.

Director: What sort of person is likely to put forth a bold hypothesis?

Scientist: Someone who believes.

Director: Believes in what?

Scientist: That they'll get lucky.

Director: And if they do get lucky?

Scientist: Then it will seem as if the discovery was destined to be made.

Director: Success erases the traces of luck?

Scientist: That's a funny way to put it. But I suppose it's true.

Director: What sort of hypotheses do you work with, Scientist?

Scientist: Ten safe bets for every one that's bold.

Director: So you hedge.

Scientist: I do. But oh, how I admire those who don't!

SEEDS (FRIEND)

Friend: Destiny is a seed you plant and nurture.

Director: And if the plant that grows from the seed dies?

Friend: Well, I suppose it means you've lost your destiny.

Director: If you lose your destiny, can you just plant another seed and try again?

Friend: That all depends on what we think the seed is, whether we have another.

Director: What is the seed?

Friend: I think it's something you believe about yourself.

Director: And after having a seed die, you might not have anything else to believe in?

Friend: Right.

Director: What if someone else plants a seed in you?

Friend: You mean someone else gives me something to believe in about myself?

Director: Yes. Do you think that ever happens?

Friend: I think it does. But I think it's more like this. Another can show you a seed you already have but just don't know you do.

Director: So seeds always come from within?

Friend: Yes.

Director: But if someone shows us a seed in ourselves, do you know what that means?

Friend: Tell me.

Director: That person knows us better than we know ourselves. Do you think that's possible?

Friend: I do. Some people don't know themselves very well. And some people are very wise when it comes to others.

Director: Now let me ask one last question. Does it matter who saw the seed first?

Friend: Of course not. What matters is that it grows.

SIGNS (ARTIST)

Artist: There's always a degree of foreshadowing involved with any destiny.

Director: So if you learn to see the signs you can predict what the destiny will be?

Artist: Yes.

Director: But, Artist, with art foreshadowing is a technique. What is it with life?

Artist: An inevitability.

Director: Can you say more?

Artist: Of course. Tell me, Director. Do you think destinies just happen out of nowhere? Or do you think they're built, steadily?

Director: I don't know.

Artist: You don't know? How can you not know?

Director: Maybe you should tell me how destiny works.

Artist: Destinies are forged, page by page, so to speak.

Director: But what if on the next page there's a great and unexpected event that changes your life?

Artist: Yes, but if you've been reading the signs up to this point, you can have a good idea as to how the character in question will react.

Director: But do you really believe that great and unexpected events can't change us in great and unexpected ways? It's all just as neat as reading what's written in a book?

Artist: Look. Events can change us — but not in a way that isn't foreseeable. And I can prove that point by playing the prophet and describing all the possible changes before the change occurs. Given such and such an event, these are the ways in which so and so might react.

Director: But isn't there all the difference in the world between knowing all that's possible and knowing what will happen in fact? Isn't the latter what prophecy is?

Artist: Prophecy is more of an art. When you've seen the signs, and you know what's possible, you'll know what's likely. And when you know what's likely, you can guess.

CREATION (SCIENTIST)

Scientist: Sometimes data present themselves and you can't for the life of you figure out why.

Director: I suppose that keeps science interesting.

Scientist: Oh, yes. Definitely.

Director: What would it mean if there ever came a day when there were no more curious data?

Scientist: When all the data just fall in line with what we think, with what we know?

Director: Yes.

Scientist: That would be the end of science.

Director: Isn't that what you want?

Scientist: The ability to explain everything? Sure.

Director: You don't sound very enthusiastic.

Scientist: I don't because that can't be what we've worked for all these years — to simply be able to say, Yes, we know why everything is the way it is.

Director: It can't?

Scientist: No, Director.

Director: Why not?

Scientist: The destiny of science can be greater than that.

Director: What can it be?

Scientist: To teach us enough in order to... create.

Director: Create a whole new world?

Scientist: Yes!

Director: And who will rule this whole new world?

Scientist: The ones who know it best.

EXPECTATION (FRIEND)

Friend: Do you think it's possible to live a life in which nothing unexpected happens?

Director: Are we talking about big things or little things?

Friend: Big things.

Director: And are these big things good or bad?

Friend: Let's say they're good.

Director: Well, if someone expects big good things to happen, and then things like that happen, nothing unexpected has happened.

Friend: But if that person expects these things to happen, and then they don't?

Director: Then the unexpected has happened, so to speak.

Friend: I think a lot of people just wait around expecting big and good things to happen. And then they're surprised.

Director: Do they think the big and good is their destiny?

Friend: Yes, I think they do. But they never do anything to bring it about.

Director: Would it be better if they didn't expect anything?

Friend: And then whatever happens is a surprise, even if it's nothing?

Director: Yes. Are surprises so bad?

Friend: No. But we all want good surprises.

Director: Even those who expect the good?

Friend: Well, no — you have a point.

Director: So tell me. If you expect the good, how can you bring it about? Do you simply live in accord with your idea of goodness, and then good things will necessarily come your way?

Friend: But that's the thing! There's no guarantee that good will come of goodness. And when it doesn't — that's the greatest surprise of all.

The Stars (Artist)

Artist: They say our destinies are written in the stars.

Director: Are they right?

Artist: How would I know? I can't read the stars. Can you?

Director: No. But isn't the notion quite poetic?

Artist: What's poetic about reading the stars?

Director: Well, do you agree poetry is a thing of beauty that's not understood by all?

Artist: Of course. Not everyone can appreciate all poetry.

Director: And not everyone can appreciate the beauty of the stars?

Artist: Assuming something is in fact written in the stars? Sure.

Director: So there it is. What's written in the stars is beautiful though not universally appreciated or understood. It's poetry.

Artist: Ha! That's the worst argument I've heard you make. But how do you know what's written there is beautiful?

Director: Beauty is in the eye of the beholder. Isn't that how it is with what you create?

Artist: Yes, but I want that beholding eye to appreciate and understand.

Director: Do you want every eye to appreciate and understand?

Artist: Why does it matter if I want that or not? Not everyone appreciates and understands. It is what it is.

Director: And that's how it is with the stars.

Artist: A writing that's there for all to see — but not all can see?

Director: Yes. And what if I tell you that even though I can't understand what's written there, I think the stars are beautiful nonetheless?

Artist: Ha! Now I know you're teasing me. So don't tell me my poetry is beautiful even though you can't see what it means. Because if you can't see it, and you still think it's beautiful, you suffer from an illusion, my friend — an illusion I want to dispel!

GAMES (SCIENTIST)

Scientist: If computers become powerful enough they could look at the whole universe as if it were an enormous game of chess.

Director: But against whom would they play?

Scientist: That's a good question. Some think it's humanity's destiny to lose the game to its own creation.

Director: What, extinction?

Scientist: Or what might be worse. Slavery.

Director: Well, we'd better be prepared to take measures.

Scientist: What measures do you think we can take?

Director: Maybe we can play the computers off of each other.

Scientist: How would we do that?

Director: The same way people do it with people.

Scientist: How?

Director: For one, we can tell one computer one thing and tell another something else.

Scientist: So they work at cross purposes? That might work. How else?

Director: Well, I suppose we can take it further. We can tell one computer that another was saying bad things about it — talking trash, as they say.

Scientist: But doesn't that assume computers will have emotions that we can play on?

Director: Who knows? Maybe they will. I just think the key is feeding them bad data in hopes they'll turn on one another — or even upon themselves.

Scientist: Suppose there are two of these computers. And then suppose we succeed in turning them against each other. And one of them wins, destroys the other. What then?

Director: I don't have an easy answer. We may need to make more computers to keep the winner occupied, so it doesn't occupy itself with us! But if we can't do that for some reason? Then I think we might be forced to invent a better game than chess, one that's rigged so computers always lose — but always love to play.

Freedom (Friend)

Friend: If we're destined for something, can we really be free?

Director: Of course we can. We're free to embrace our destiny or not.

Friend: What happens if we don't embrace our destiny?

Director: The something in question might not happen.

Friend: And then we're left to our fate?

Director: Well, that's an interesting question for you to raise.

Friend: Why?

Director: Because it implies the only true choice we have is one between destiny and fate.

Friend: Do you believe that's our only real choice?

Director: I find it hard to say it's not.

Friend: Well, I think it boils down to a fundamental yes or no.

Director: Destiny is the yes, while fate is the no?

Friend: Of course.

Director: But what if we say yes to fate?

Friend: I don't see why we would. Fate just happens anyway, if we deny our destiny.

Director: Does that make fate the more powerful of the two?

Friend: Now that's an interesting question. I want to say no, but something urges me to say yes.

Director: Why?

Friend: Because it takes an effort to break away from fate.

Director: But no effort at all to break with destiny?

Friend: Yes, I think that's exactly it. And I think that's true for freedom, too. It takes so much to be free, but so little to become... enslaved.

Artificial (Artist)

Artist: Why would you ask me? I'm not a scientist. I have no idea what artificial intelligence is.

Director: Isn't it just intelligence we create?

Artist: Sure, but every baby that's born is intelligence we create.

Director: Maybe artificial intelligence just means non-human intelligence.

Artist: But what if we implant non-human intelligent devices into humans to make their native intelligence more intelligent? Is that human or artificial?

Director: I suppose it's both, a hybrid. But do you think it's the same thing if we alter the genetics before conception to produce more intelligence?

Artist: Well, then that intelligence is truly native.

Director: If artificially native?

Artist: Sure. But don't animal breeders do the same thing naturally?

Director: You mean if they breed for intelligence?

Artist: Yes. Is that breeding natural or artificial?

Director: I don't know. But couldn't we ask the same questions about human mating practices?

Artist: You mean if humans mate based on intelligence in hopes of producing highly intelligent offspring? That's as natural as it gets.

Director: So there's an art, an art of choice, even in the natural? Just as there's art in everything that's artificial?

Artist: No doubt. So what are you saying? That things natural and things artificial aren't all that far apart?

Director: Ah, I thought I could count on you to point to that conclusion. After all, isn't art destined to try to resolve its dispute with nature?

Artist: True, Director. And when the resolution is good, very good — it seems like it was meant to be.

GOOD DEEDS (SCIENTIST)

Scientist: Can we shape our destiny by doing good deeds? I'm inclined to say yes.

Director: What kind of destiny would we shape with such deeds?

Scientist: A good destiny.

Director: Because what goes around comes around?

Scientist: Yes, in so many words.

Director: So if we do a great many small good deeds, we can expect to have a great many small good deeds done to us?

Scientist: Not necessarily. We might get back one great big good deed instead.

Director: Does that mean things work the other way, as well?

Scientist: How do you mean?

Director: If we do one great big good deed, we might get back many small good deeds.

Scientist: Yes, I think that's true.

Director: But what if the opposite happens? What if good deeds, large or small, bring bad deeds in return?

Scientist: Well, I'm not sure it actually works that way. The bad deeds might just happen on their own and not be in return for the good.

Director: But if that's true, couldn't we say the same thing, and with equal validity, about good deeds?

Scientist: You mean they just happen to us on their own and aren't connected in any way to our prior good deeds?

Director: Yes. What do you think?

Scientist: If that's how it is, then nothing makes sense!

Director: But good deeds are still good deeds and leave a legacy of good. No?

Scientist: Yes. But it's not enough to leave a legacy of good. You need to enjoy it, too.

Bad Deeds (Friend)

Friend: There's no doubt that bad deeds will shape your destiny.

Director: Just as there's no doubt that good deeds will, too?

Friend: I think it's different.

Director: Why?

Friend: Because of the difference in nature between the two.

Director: What's the nature of each?

Friend: Good deeds help others. Bad deeds do harm.

Director: So why is there no doubt about bad deeds but there is doubt about good?

Friend: People never forget a harm. But people are often ungrateful when it comes to something good. And the ungrateful forget.

Director: But then what are we saying? That the remembering and forgetting of others is what gives shape to our lives?

Friend: In large part? Yes.

Director: Hmm. I don't think I like this very much.

Friend: Why not?

Director: Don't most people want to be remembered?

Friend: True.

Director: Well, if harming others guarantees you'll be remembered — are we saying most people want to do harm?

Friend: Of course not! It matters what you're remembered for, not just that you're remembered at all.

Director: So most people want to persuade others to remember their good?

Friend: Yes. And here's a trick that helps. When we're cooking up our good, we can spice it with a touch, just the tiniest pinch, of something wicked, something bad — completely harmless, of course. And then people remember the meal!

Irresponsibility (Artist)

Artist: Destiny is liberating, for those who have a destiny.

Director: Unlike you? But in what sense does it liberate?

Artist: In the sense that you're not responsible for your destiny.

Director: Opinions vary on that, you know.

Artist: Of course I do. But my opinion is that destiny is nothing you can control.

Director: But you have another opinion, don't you?

Artist: What opinion is that?

Director: That if you have a destiny then everything you do toward that end you're destined to do.

Artist: You know me very well! So now you can draw the conclusion.

Director: I'd rather hear it from you.

Artist: Alright. If everything we do for destiny's sake we're destined to do, and we're not responsible for our destiny, then we're completely free of responsibility for anything we do toward destiny's end! What do you think?

Director: I think that's terrible.

Artist: What? Don't you think the conclusion follows necessarily from the premises? Or do you think one or more of the premises is false?

Director: I'm not interested in sparring logic with you, Artist. I just want to know one thing.

Artist: Oh? What?

Director: Do you keep these thoughts to yourself and only share them with friends like me? Or do you own up to them with one and all?

Artist: Ha! You know there are constraints in voicing opinions like this.

Director: So you don't believe in preaching this perfect license of yours?

Artist: I don't believe in being held responsible — for preaching no responsibility at all!

Way of the Wise (Scientist)

Scientist: We must know our destiny and live up to it.

Director: As a responsibility?

Scientist: As an absolute responsibility.

Director: If that's so, then we should consider each of the parts of that whole closely.

Scientist: What do you mean?

Director: Just that each part — the knowledge of destiny and the living up to it — must be right or the whole thing is wrong. Do you agree?

Scientist: Certainly.

Director: So how do we know our destiny?

Scientist: The way we know anything.

Director: We formulate hypotheses and then conduct experiments?

Scientist: Yes, I like that. But it's funny. I never applied my method to my own destiny.

Director: Is that because you already knew your destiny before you came to science?

Scientist: I knew science was for me just as I began.

Director: But if not through scientific method, then how did you come to know?

Scientist: This may sound strange. But I came to know in the way we come to wisdom.

Director: You mean to say you just knew without being able to explain exactly how?

Scientist: Yes. It was a feeling I had. A certainty.

Director: So there are two ways to know? First through science and then through what we can call the way of the wise?

Scientist: Precisely. But that's the easy part. What's hard is living up to what we know.

Director: Really? I think many struggle greatly in order to know their destiny, to know what's meant to be. And for them, who knows? Maybe once they know, living up to their destiny proves to be a relief.

Immaterial (Friend)

Friend: But what if it doesn't matter whether we believe in destiny or not?

Director: Why wouldn't it?

Friend: Because whatever happens, happens. Does it really matter that something happens because of destiny?

Director: You mean what's the point of destiny? What if it serves no purpose? And yet many believe in destiny. Maybe their very belief is the purpose?

Friend: You mean the purpose of destiny is to give them something to believe in? Then here's how I think it goes. People start out wanting something, and a belief in destiny gives them hope that they'll get what they want.

Director: So if someone aspires to be some sort of great leader, for instance, the belief that it's their destiny to become that leader gives them hope that they one day will?

Friend: Yes. But can't someone just hope to be the leader without getting destiny involved? Do you know what I mean?

Director: I do. But it doesn't seem everyone can do that.

Friend: Well, maybe believing it's their destiny to be something makes them more confident and that makes them better able to do the things they must do in order to become what they want to be.

Director: I wonder if that's the purpose of all belief.

Friend: To make us more confident? Sure. But then we're not accounting for negative beliefs. But what do you think? If we meet people who lack confidence, should we just give them something good to believe?

Director: That seems too cynical. Can't we give them something good to know, not just believe?

Friend: What, like the truth about themselves?

Director: Yes. But, Friend, isn't that truth hard for us to say and harder for them to hear — assuming we're sure we know the truth, which is no small assumption?

Friend: Is it hard? Not necessarily. Not if that truth is something we know they'll be eager to hear. And I have to believe that happens, at times.

CONTROL (ARTIST)

Artist: Would you have control over someone if you somehow knew their destiny?

Director: Count on you to ask that question.

Artist: No, but seriously! What do you think?

Director: Are you asking about knowing someone's destiny, or knowing what someone believes is their destiny?

Artist: Ah, very subtle. The latter.

Director: You'd manipulate them based on their belief?

Artist: Yes, like a true artist.

Director: And toward what end?

Artist: Why, the good!

Director: I wonder what you mean by 'good'. Is it good to let people go on believing in their destiny under such circumstances, under your influence?

Artist: It depends on the people.

Director: What kind would you encourage to go on in their belief?

Artist: Why, those whose belief is for the good.

Director: And who would you attempt to disillusion?

Artist: Everybody else.

Director: But how do you know whose belief is for the good?

Artist: Oh, Director. You always have to plod along. Don't you know? It's always good for someone else to set their sights very, very high.

Director: High enough that it's impossible?

Artist: Ha! No, impossible isn't good.

Director: What would you do if you had set your sights that high?

Artist: Me? On the impossible? I'd do the hardest thing in the world. I'd lower my aim.

Worlds (Scientist)

Scientist: Well, I suppose if science somehow came to know the world's destiny, it could then turn to trying to find a way out.

Director: You mean it could try to find other, alternative destinies?

Scientist: Precisely.

Director: But then once found, who's to say which destiny is best?

Scientist: I suppose we could put it to a vote.

Director: So the majority gets the world it wants?

Scientist: That's the problem.

Director: The problem for the minorities?

Scientist: Of course. But if you want my honest opinion, we must do everything we can to protect the minorities.

Director: So what can we do? Give the minorities their own alternative world destinies?

Scientist: I know what you're saying. But that's not possible. The world is the world. And that's why we have to create colonies.

Director: Colonies on other worlds?

Scientist: Yes, but we must all stay closely in touch. Because science, in order to thrive, must have a constant stream of alternative views.

Director: And science would help nurture these views, if only in order to sustain itself?

Scientist: Yes.

Director: So what are we really saying here, Scientist? That science would help birth a variety of destinies, or points of view, by making possible worlds in which to live them?

Scientist: That's what we're saying.

Director: Then surely you must know what the most important question is.

Scientist: Of course I do. How can science obtain the power it needs to do what must be done?

Adding Up (Friend)

Friend: I suppose if you knew your destiny you'd be at peace.

Director: Once you accepted it?

Friend: Yes.

Director: What stops you from accepting your destiny?

Friend: It might not be the destiny you thought was yours.

Director: You mean you believed in a certain destiny?

Friend: Yes, without truly knowing it was yours.

Director: How do you know your destiny?

Friend: Everything adds up that way.

Director: What if something doesn't add up?

Friend: You'll never rest easy until you figure it out.

Director: And if no matter how hard you try, it just won't add up?

Friend: Then you know you're wrong.

Director: Do you think someone can help you with this?

Friend: I think it's best if you can figure it out on your own. But I also think it's better to figure it out with help rather than never to figure it out at all.

Director: To whom would you turn for help?

Friend: To someone who's good with the figures of destiny, naturally. And, just as importantly, to someone with a gentle touch.

Director: Why a gentle touch?

Friend: Director, we're talking about someone's destiny here. That's as delicate a topic as there is. It just won't do to have someone stomping around like a bull.

Director: Yes, egos can be fragile, my friend. But who says destiny itself is any such thing?

Measuring Up (Artist)

Artist: I wouldn't want to know my destiny if I could.

Director: Why not?

Artist: I want the unknown in my life. Don't you?

Director: But can't you know your destiny and not know if you're living up to it?

Artist: Bah. People say that. But if you know your destiny you know full well if you're living up to it or not.

Director: How?

Artist: Am I the best one to ask? I don't even want to know my destiny, let alone whether I'm measuring up!

Director: But you still think people somehow know?

Artist: Yes, certainly. They have an idea in their head, and if their deeds are in harmony with the theme of the idea? Viola! Destiny achieved.

Director: But you don't mean that. You mean destiny on track to being achieved.

Artist: No, I mean achieved.

Director: How so?

Artist: If you live up to an idea, however briefly, you've achieved success, however limited.

Director: You surprise me.

Artist: Why? You think I'm letting them off too easily?

Director: Well, yes.

Artist: It's because I think it's impossible to fully live up to an idea of destiny, or any idea for that matter. The best someone can do is live up to it at times, for moments.

Director: And so you don't bother to try to fully live up to anything? Not even in your art?

Artist: My art? My art lives up to the highest possible standards! But as for me? I'm not so vain.

Reactions (Scientist)

Scientist: The unknown will always be.

Director: Why?

Scientist: Because even if we know what will happen, we don't know how we'll react to it when it happens.

Director: And doesn't it go the other way, too? I mean, we won't know how we'll react to knowing what will happen.

Scientist: True. Ultimately, reactions are unknowable.

Director: But don't reactions partially determine subsequent happenings?

Scientist: Well, yes. That's why if we hope to predict the future, we would need to be able to predict reactions.

Director: In order that the unknown no longer be. But you think that's impossible?

Scientist: Of course. It's an infinite problem, as you suggested. How will someone react to knowing what their reaction will be? And if they know that, how will they react to that? And so on. We'll never chase down what the final reaction will be.

Director: And that final reaction might influence all the rest and so we'd have to start all over again, predicting and predicting?

Scientist: Unless we know and don't tell what people's reactions will be.

Director: You mean we just let them react?

Scientist: Yes. We leave their reactions to whatever nature destined them to be.

Director: But then we have an unfair advantage. We know what they don't know.

Scientist: What would make it fair?

Director: Sharing what we know, as much as we know — if in fact we know.

Scientist: But that's the thing. If we share, we'll never know if we knew. The sharing changes the reaction pattern the whole way down the line.

Director: You'd rather know than be fair? I didn't know how dedicated to science you were, my friend.

CHOICE (FRIEND)

Friend: So we can either accept our destiny or reject it. And that's the only true freedom we have.

Director: Yes, that's what we're saying.

Friend: But how can we be sure?

Director: Well, have you tried rejecting your destiny?

Friend: I don't know what my destiny is!

Director: Ah, then let me let you in on a secret: that's the best kind of rejection there is.

Friend: Why would you say that?

Director: Because when you know your destiny, when you have more than just some hazy idea, and you're honest with yourself — you'll feel you have no real choice but to accept.

Friend: But what if I don't have a destiny?

Director: Oh, I think you do.

Friend: How would you know?

Director: It's my destiny to know these things.

Friend: I can't tell if you're being serious or teasing me. So tell me what my destiny is.

Director: Are you sure you want to know?

Friend: If I know I really must accept?

Director: You can try to fight it. Many do. But that's not a good way to live.

Friend: Can't I know and then decide?

Director: Decide whether or not to fight what you know?

Friend: I think you're mocking me. You don't know my destiny. Do you?

Director: I know more than what you think, but less than what you fear. So think on that, and then decide if you'd like to hear what I have to say.

HEROES (ARTIST)

Artist: I think true heroes war against their destiny.

Director: Why?

Artist: Because they want to be free.

Director: What greater freedom is there than in living your destiny?

Artist: Yes, yes. But when you're living it, you're in harness.

Director: You mean you don't feel free.

Artist: Not at all. At least not at first.

Director: So how do you portray freedom in art?

Artist: You show the hero slipping out of harness.

Director: And then?

Artist: The hero tries to live without destiny — but misses the great sense of purpose.

Director: So the hero comes to believe that freedom is a lie?

Artist: For a certain time.

Director: And then?

Artist: And then the hero learns what you said. What greater freedom than destiny?

Director: This is a classic theme for art, isn't it?

Artist: None more classic than that.

Director: Learning how your harness makes you free. Well, you surprise me once again, Artist.

Artist: Oh? Why is that?

Director: Because you're harnessed to your art. So what does that make you?

Artist: Ha! Well, while every hero has a harness, not every harness makes a hero. And that, my friend, is all I've got to say.

Learning (Scientist)

Scientist: Learn what you're good at. Surely that's part of your destiny.

Director: Yes, I would think so. But how do you learn?

Scientist: You try different things and get a sense for what goes well with you.

Director: But what if what you're meant to be good at doesn't go well with you at first?

Scientist: You might give up — and miss out on your calling.

Director: So what should you do? Keep trying and trying? Even if it means beating your head against the wall?

Scientist: I know what you're saying. I think that for destiny there will be a sign.

Director: A sign? That doesn't sound very scientific. Can you say more?

Scientist: Let me put it another way. There will be evidence.

Director: Evidence that, though you might flounder at first, this is your thing?

Scientist: Don't you agree?

Director: I'm inclined to say yes. But what if there's only a very small clue?

Scientist: The destined always look out for even the smallest of clues.

Director: Why?

Scientist: Because they all start out as hunters, seekers for what's properly theirs.

Director: And those who lack that instinct to hunt aren't destined at all?

Scientist: I'm afraid not. Not in the least.

Director: Not even if a great big pile of evidence appears before their very eyes?

Scientist: As a scientist I know that evidence alone just isn't enough. It takes someone who knows what to make of it all.

Director: And only the destined will know?

Scientist: Only the destined will take the trouble to see these things for what they truly are.

Learning (Friend)

Friend: Learn what you're no good at — because then you know your destiny doesn't lead that way.

Director: So a process of elimination is best? But how do you know what to try and eliminate? I mean out of so many things in the world, how do you know what to choose?

Friend: Go with what interests you.

Director: So you try to eliminate the things that interest you? That doesn't sound quite right.

Friend: But what else can you do? You have to see if you're good at something. And if you're not, then you eliminate.

Director: But what if you eliminate everything you're interested in? Do you then start to try things you're not interested in?

Friend: I suppose you don't have much choice.

Director: But how likely are you to find something you're good at among things you're not interested in?

Friend: Maybe you don't know you're interested. I mean, maybe you get lucky and find you're good at something you don't really care for at first, but you learn to like this thing over time, to take an interest in it.

Director: But if you don't care for it, why would you learn to like it?

Friend: Because it's a shame not to like what you're good at.

Director: Fear of shame makes you learn to like what you're good at?

Friend: No, of course not. It's simply in our nature to like, to take a real interest in, these things.

Director: And yet not everyone does. Why?

Friend: I suppose they have other priorities. And these priorities go against nature.

Director: How in the world do people learn to have priorities like that?

Friend: Director, I wish I knew.

EQUALITY (ARTIST)

Artist: Are all destinies equal? No, of course not.

Director: You mean a humble destiny can't be as good as an illustrious destiny?

Artist: Do you think it can?

Director: I don't know, Artist. I'm not sure how illustrious my own destiny is, and yet I think it's worth living out.

Artist: Yes, yes — many destinies are worth living out. But not all destinies are equal.

Director: Not equal in the sense that one is better than another? Or not equal in the sense that an apple isn't equal to an orange?

Artist: Both.

Director: How both?

Artist: Apples and oranges aren't equal, as you say. Sure, they're both fruits, destinies, we'll say. But if I love apples and don't care for oranges, then aren't apples better in my eyes?

Director: In your eyes, yes. So is that the way it is as concerns inequality of destinies? They're only unequal because people see them that way?

Artist: Yes, but note this. That doesn't mean they are, in some higher sense, equal. The only equality is the equality we choose to see.

Director: So there are two types of people in the world? Those who choose to see equality of destinies and those who choose to see inequality?

Artist: Yes.

Director: And you see inequality.

Artist: Absolutely.

Director: So what's the greatest contrast, the greatest inequality between two destinies?

Artist: That all depends on how much imagination you have. On how much distance you can conceive of between the sweetest and most bitter of fruits. And trust me when I say, Director, that for me — that distance is vast.

HAPPINESS (SCIENTIST)

Scientist: Let's suppose happiness is the only good.

Director: Alright. Do you have to walk with destiny in order to be happy?

Scientist: No, I don't think you do.

Director: So you can be happy either with or without destiny? Which way is better?

Scientist: I'm not sure either is better. Happiness is happiness.

Director: Then maybe I should ask — which is easier?

Scientist: Oh, I don't know that I'd say happiness is ever easy.

Director: So there's no essential difference between being destined to be happy and just being happy?

Scientist: I don't think there is.

Director: Then we're saying destiny doesn't matter? Destiny doesn't make a difference?

Scientist: I suppose we are.

Director: But that's only as far as happiness goes. I mean someone might, for example, become the greatest scientist of our century. He or she would need to be destined for that. No?

Scientist: I'm not sure. But let's suppose it's true.

Director: Not so fast. Why do you think it might not be true?

Scientist: I think you should tell me a way that it might be true.

Director: Here's one way. All greatness involves pain. Belief in your destiny makes up for the pain. In other words, walking with destiny puts pain in its place. And when the pain is in its place, well, then there's room to be great — and maybe to be happy, too.

Scientist: You know, someone could easily challenge that argument at each step along the way.

Director: Then why not offer up a better one yourself?

Scientist: Because I believe what you said is true.

MISERY (FRIEND)

Friend: What if you spend your life striving after a goal, your destiny, and you're miserable the whole time — but you achieve it?

Director: What if?

Friend: Does it make all the misery worth it?

Director: Well, I imagine it would be better than not achieving it, wouldn't it? But are there really such goals?

Friend: What do you mean?

Director: You seem to be implying this is an all or nothing matter. Aren't there stages along the way no matter the goal? I mean if you think it's your destiny to be president, do you go from being private citizen to president all in one leap?

Friend: No. You might start out as a local representative.

Director: And that's one goal achieved along the way to the big goal. Would you feel good about having achieved that goal?

Friend: You would.

Director: Would that make up for whatever misery you might have felt along the way?

Friend: In large part? Let's say it would.

Director: And it's the same if you become governor, or senator, or whatever?

Friend: Yes.

Director: So should we rethink your initial question?

Friend: No. I still think it's possible to be miserable most of the time. Sure, you might enjoy successes that make what you've done so far seem worth it. But then it's back to misery, the struggle. In the end your end goal destroys you — unless you succeed. And even then....

Director: Yes, you might still be destroyed. So what can we conclude?

Friend: That if you're mostly miserable, you've got the wrong goal. And if you've got the wrong goal, you're waging a losing war against fate.

Virtue (Artist)

Artist: Those with virtue have better destinies than those without? I don't know, Director.

Director: What don't you know?

Artist: What do you mean by 'better'?

Director: What does anyone mean by 'better'?

Artist: The next step up from good. But what do you mean?

Director: More desirable.

Artist: Virtue makes for a more desirable destiny? Ha! Do you know what I'd say?

Director: Tell me.

Artist: Virtue gets in the way of having a more desirable destiny!

Director: How does it do that?

Artist: If you're all caught up in worrying about virtue, how are you ever going to boldly seize the destiny you want?

Director: Now it's my turn to ask what you mean.

Artist: In regards to what?

Director: Virtue.

Artist: Why do you ask?

Director: Because 'virtue', as I conceive of it, is precisely what allows you to boldly seize the destiny you want — a better destiny, a more desirable destiny.

Artist: Interesting! You know that's not how I was thinking of it. I was thinking of virtue as something weak. As 'being good'.

Director: Well, now we have another topic to discuss.

Artist: What it means to be good?

Director: Yes. I think all virtue must be good. And goodness isn't weak.

Artist: Alright. But then we'll say all goodness isn't virtue. And I like what this suggests.

Discipline (Scientist)

Scientist: Here's how the reasoning goes. Science has a great destiny. Anything that supports something that has a great destiny is itself great. Discipline supports science. Therefore discipline is great.

Director: Let me ask you this. Is discipline always great?

Scientist: As far as science is concerned? Yes.

Director: What if we step outside the realm of science?

Scientist: Discipline is still always great.

Director: Is it bad if there's too little discipline?

Scientist: Yes, of course.

Director: Similarly, is it bad if there's too much discipline?

Scientist: We're still talking outside of science?

Director: Why, is it different within science?

Scientist: There's no such thing as too much discipline within science.

Director: Not even if you have so much discipline it blinds you?

Scientist: What do you mean? Prevents you from being creative?

Director: Yes.

Scientist: I suppose there's something to that. But that only occurs in the far reaches of science, Director.

Director: So it's not every day that you see too much discipline?

Scientist: No, not at all.

Director: Okay. But now let's get back to regular life. Is too much discipline possible there?

Scientist: I suppose it's the same as with science — yes, but it's rare. So I think it's best to tell everyone that there can never be too much discipline, and that great discipline supports a great destiny. And then with the ones who overdo it? We'll confide the truth.

Waiting (Friend)

Friend: Sometimes you just have to wait and let destiny take care of itself.

Director: How do you know when it's time to wait?

Friend: I think of it like this. If I'm sailing a ship at sea, and a great calm comes over the face of the deep, with not even the slightest breeze — I know it's time to wait.

Director: So you wait when you're not going anywhere, when you have nothing better to do?

Friend: In so many words, yes. But there is something important I can do while I wait.

Director: Oh? What?

Friend: I can commune with my soul.

Director: And let me guess. Destiny is never more present to you than then?

Friend: Exactly. You see your destiny all that much more clearly when you're deeply in touch with your soul.

Director: And I'll guess once more. You'll be that much more effective in following your destiny once the wind rises and you're on your way, for having communed with your soul.

Friend: Yes.

Director: So waiting can be good.

Friend: Waiting can be very good.

Director: Then why are so many people so impatient?

Friend: I think they're afraid.

Director: Of what?

Friend: Communing with their soul.

Director: But why would they be afraid of that?

Friend: Simply put? Not every soul is beautiful when beheld at length.

Rushing (Artist)

Artist: Rushing into your destiny never makes sense.

Director: Not even if you're sure what your destiny is?

Artist: No, not even then.

Director: Then how should you proceed?

Artist: You should slither and sidewind toward destiny like a snake.

Director: Really? Why is that better than rushing in?

Artist: Because you can size your destiny up from the ground.

Director: And when you go running into it, you can't?

Artist: Yes.

Director: What does it mean to size destiny up from the ground?

Artist: To study the foundation, what it requires to stand.

Director: And if you don't know that, you might accidentally knock your destiny down?

Artist: It happens all the time.

Director: So what does this mean for artists?

Artist: No attempts at great work until many studies have been made to size your subject up.

Director: How do you know when you've made enough?

Artist: Your studies themselves will border on being great.

Director: So it's a natural, almost imperceptible, transition to greatness?

Artist: That's the best kind — the safest, at least.

Director: And this holds for non-artists, too?

Artist: Of course. But there the stakes are much higher. An artist might ruin a work. But others might ruin a life.

The Facts (Scientist)

Scientist: Knowing your destiny involves taking into account all of the facts — not just the ones you like.

Director: So it's like science in that way.

Scientist: Yes. And that's why I'm persuaded that people should take a scientific approach to their destiny.

Director: But is our destiny any less our destiny if we don't take a scientific approach?

Scientist: Destiny is destiny, sure. But if we're not scientific toward it, we won't know it very well.

Director: Not even if we know it in the way of wisdom?

Scientist: Wisdom is a special case.

Director: I see. But let's get back to science and an example. Am I less certain I'm a very bad basketball player because I wasn't scientific in coming to that conclusion?

Scientist: How did you come to the conclusion?

Director: Every time I played I was horrible.

Scientist: But that could have been scientific. Each game played was an experiment testing the hypothesis that you're a good player. The evidence mounted and you concluded the hypothesis is false.

Director: So everything that everyone does is, in a way, science?

Scientist: No. Some people are bad at basketball and think they're good. That's not science.

Director: It's only science when you're right?

Scientist: Precisely.

Director: Hmm. But what if instead of playing against good players I play against bad players — and they make me look good? Could science draw the wrong conclusion?

Scientist: Yes. But that's why it needs to know the game and not just the facts.

Director: Then let's hope someone who knows it well will teach science the game.

Fools (Friend)

Friend: Fools believe what others tell them about their destiny.

Director: You mean you have to come up with your destiny on your own?

Friend: Yes. That's the only way.

Director: Why?

Friend: Because otherwise you can be misled.

Director: Misled as in told something is your destiny when it's not? But why would anyone do that?

Friend: One, because they sincerely believe they know your destiny even though they don't. Two, because they want to take advantage of you. And do you know when either of these ways is hardest to resist?

Director: Tell me.

Friend: When the person misleading you is a close family member or friend.

Director: I see. But if you do resist what they tell you, how will you seem to them?

Friend: Well, if they truly believe what they're telling you is true, they'll probably think you're a fool.

Director: And if they're trying to take advantage of you?

Friend: They'll think you see right through them.

Director: And seeing right through them wouldn't be very foolish at all, would it?

Friend: Not at all.

Director: So tell me, Friend. Is there ever a time when you can believe what someone tells you about your destiny? A time when it would be foolish not to believe?

Friend: Yes, of course. When what they tell you squares with what you've already arrived at on your own concerning your own destined way.

Director: But what if you've made a mistake?

Friend: Then you have to hope no one tells you only what you want to hear.

Alone (Artist)

Artist: We all reach our destinies alone.

Director: What if our destiny is to be with others?

Artist: Yes, yes. But even when we're with others we're alone.

Director: Aren't you taking all the meaning out of the word 'alone'?

Artist: Am I? I'm with you now but I'm still alone.

Director: Do you mean to say you're independent of me?

Artist: Yes.

Director: But you can be independent and not be alone.

Artist: But I am alone.

Director: What would make you not be alone?

Artist: With you? Right now? Sharing my innermost thoughts.

Director: Do you ever share your innermost thoughts?

Artist: When I'm with others? No. But I do share them in a way through my work.

Director: Why don't you want to be like your work?

Artist: Because my work can take it and I can't.

Director: Take it? You mean you're vulnerable?

Artist: I am — as are we all, Director.

Director: So we're all alone, except for when we express our innermost thoughts. But we're so vulnerable our only hope for such expression is with art? But many of us have no art.

Artist: Oh, we all have our art. That's how we express ourselves every day. You don't need a book, painting, or score to be an artist. You just need to exercise some craft in everyday life. And if you're lucky, there will be those who understand what you do. But don't get too close. It's best if you keep some distance from them. After all, you're in it, as far as destiny goes — all on your own.

TOGETHER (SCIENTIST)

Scientist: We can travel together to our destiny as a people, as the world!

Director: What's gotten into you? You sound like you're drunk.

Scientist: Ha, ha! But seriously. Don't you think that's true?

Director: Scientist, are you suggesting that all peoples have the same destiny as the entire world?

Scientist: No, of course not. But don't you think that all rivers flow into the sea?

Director: Mostly. But what if someone would rather be a lake?

Scientist: Why do you want to resist the destiny of the world?

Director: Someone has to resist.

Scientist: Why?

Director: Because what if that destiny is no good?

Scientist: But do you really think one person's resistance can change all that? How?

Director: By encouraging others to be lakes, deep lakes.

Scientist: And if there are enough deep lakes, what happens to the sea?

Director: Oh, I think the sea can take care of itself.

Scientist: If the sea is the sea, what good are the lakes?

Director: Lakes are good for those who want to be themselves.

Scientist: You can't be yourself in the sea?

Director: You can. But you'd have to be quite strong. And what in the world is more rare than strength?

Scientist: But what are you saying? To be a lake takes less strength than being yourself in the sea?

Director: No. It takes the greatest of strength to leave the ocean, go back up stream, become a fine lake — and harbor no ill will toward those of the sea.

PRAISE AND BAD LUCK (FRIEND)

Friend: Should we praise people for living out their destiny?

Director: That assumes we know their destiny.

Friend: Let's suppose we somehow do.

Director: Alright. Is this a good destiny or a bad destiny that we want to praise?

Friend: A good destiny.

Director: Why not a bad destiny?

Friend: Who would want to praise a bad destiny?

Director: Ah, I can see you're not very sophisticated when it comes to these things.

Friend: What are you talking about?

Director: Some of the sophisticated praise those who have bad destinies — in order to tempt them toward the abyss.

Friend: What, like a sort of mercy killing?

Director: Yes, but without the mercy.

Friend: But what if the bad destiny is simply due to bad luck?

Director: We're not to blame for our bad luck?

Friend: Of course we're not!

Director: But don't people blame those with bad luck all the time?

Friend: Yes, that's true. But they think the people they blame had a choice.

Director: Is that what they think? I think some of them don't care whether there were choices or not, even if only for the lesser of two evils.

Friend: But then they're not fair.

Director: Does that surprise you?

Friend: No. But it makes me wish bad luck on them.

NECESSITY (ARTIST)

Artist: Destiny is a sort of necessity.

Director: In what sense?

Artist: In the sense that it compels you along your way.

Director: So unless you feel that compulsion, you're not living your destiny?

Artist: Yes. What do you think?

Director: Well, let me ask. Are there other things in life that can compel you?

Artist: There are.

Director: So how can you be sure it's destiny compelling you and not something else?

Artist: Because nothing else compels you on your way. The way is what counts.

Director: So you need to recognize your way if you're to know what's happening to you?

Artist: No doubt.

Director: Then how do you recognize your way?

Artist: It has a unique dual character. The way is at once both comforting and frightening.

Director: That's an unusual combination. Are you sure that's how it is?

Artist: Yes, yes — of course. It's comforting in that it takes away the agony of choice. And it's frightening because it leaves you with no choice.

Director: No choice but to keep moving on your way — crawl or walk or run?

Artist: That's right. Destiny just keeps pushing you along.

Director: What if you resist?

Artist: It's like trying to stand still by treading water in a fast-moving stream.

Director: But what if you swim to the bank and climb on out?

Artist: Ah, Director, tell me. Who, when pushed along by the waters of destiny, would ever want to get out — and join the likes of me?

Peace (Scientist)

Scientist: The destiny of democracy, Director, is to be universal and to enjoy worldwide peace.

Director: How do you know that? I mean, couldn't democracy become universal and suffer from chronic war?

Scientist: Why would it?

Director: I don't know. But it's possible, no?

Scientist: I suppose. But what are you suggesting?

Director: What do you mean?

Scientist: Are you suggesting there's a type of rule more conducive to peace?

Director: What, you mean like kingship or aristocracy? In our age? No, I wasn't trying to suggest that.

Scientist: Regardless, do you think that with one of those forms of government, or one derived from them, even if only in part — peace is more likely on a global scale?

Director: Oh, Scientist. How could I possibly say? It all depends.

Scientist: On what?

Director: The state of the globe.

Scientist: When would world peace require something like a king?

Director: Why are you asking me this? Isn't it obvious that it would be when one firm will is needed to keep the peace?

Scientist: And when something like an aristocracy?

Director: When a minority of coordinated wills is what it takes to do the same, to beat back the flames.

Scientist: And when democracy, in your opinion?

Director: A pure and direct democracy? When collective wisdom shows it's truly wise. Assuming, of course, that wisdom always calls for peace.

PRINCES AND KINGS (FRIEND)

Friend: What's the destiny of princes and kings? Well, I think they've changed form.

Director: How so?

Friend: We now have presidents, and chief executives, and chairmen, and majority shareholders, and so on, and so on.

Director: I'm not sure it's the same sort of thing, Friend.

Friend: Why not?

Director: These people are all still accountable to the law. And they don't have absolute power and rule for life.

Friend: Yes, they're accountable to the law — in theory. And as for absolute power and rule for life? Even real princes and kings didn't always have such power and rule.

Director: Yes, but what about heredity?

Friend: You've got me there — except in the case of family owned businesses and certain clans that have come to dominate our politics.

Director: If these people are so like princes and kings, why aren't they content?

Friend: I think deep down inside, they want a title, too.

Director: Really? And how would they get this?

Friend: By election, of course.

Director: Wouldn't it be a sign of real trouble if we elected someone prince or king?

Friend: Not if most people thought someone were truly fit to rule.

Director: I don't know, Friend. What would such a person be like?

Friend: Strong. Strong in everything. Strong in heart. Strong in mind. Strong in friendship. Strong in courage. And so on, and so on.

Director: Hmm. Tell me. Would people be willing to fight for someone like this?

Friend: Fight? No, Director. They wouldn't. But they'd fight for what this prince or king stands for — in them.

Aristocracies, Democracies (Artist)

Artist: Aristocracies are destined to always exist.

Director: Why do you say that?

Artist: Well, tell me. What does 'aristocracy' mean?

Director: Rule of the few or rule of the best, depending who you ask.

Artist: Let's say it's the few. Even in democracies the few always rule.

Director: Do you mean the wealthy?

Artist: Yes.

Director: But then it's not really a democracy.

Artist: When is it ever a democracy?

Director: When the people rule.

Artist: Ha! And what do you think that would look like? True democracy, I mean.

Director: Are you asking me about direct democracy?

Artist: Yes. No representatives or other go-betweens — just the people's rule.

Director: Well, I suppose we'd have to vote on all national actions.

Artist: Like when it's time to go to war?

Director: Yes.

Artist: Do you want a worked up mob voting on when to go to war?

Director: I wouldn't want a worked up mob voting on anything. But why do you assume there would be a mob?

Artist: Because people vote their interests. And when interests clash, there's trouble. Trouble leads to frothing at the mouth. And when many mouths froth I call it a mob.

Director: And so you prefer the rule of the few?

Artist: I prefer the few to labor within democracy's fold. Because when they rule openly, they usually become nothing better than a mob of their own.

TRAGEDIES (SCIENTIST)

Scientist: Ideally? Science does away with tragedy. But, of course, there will always be the tragedy of those who resist science.

Director: How does science do away with tragedy?

Scientist: By coming to know the grounds of tragedy — and doing away with them.

Director: And those who resist science, they resist because they don't want to lose their grounds?

Scientist: Yes.

Director: Tell me. Are there two types of tragedy?

Scientist: What two types do you have in mind?

Director: Public and private.

Scientist: Yes, I think that's fair to say.

Director: Which is easier to combat?

Scientist: For science? The public.

Director: Why?

Scientist: How easy do you think it is for science to get into the private lives of individuals?

Director: Not very?

Scientist: Yes. So you see? Science starts with the public.

Director: In hopes of penetrating the private.

Scientist: Yes. After all, if the public goes one way...

Director: ...the private must one day, too?

Scientist: Of course.

Director: But that assumes private individuals will surrender themselves to science. No?

Scientist: Surrender or not. What we really assume — is that there will be no choice.

COMEDY (FRIEND)

Friend: I'd like to have a comic destiny.

Director: Why?

Friend: It's better than having a tragic destiny.

Director: What signs would there be that your destiny is comic?

Friend: I'd be able to take things lightly.

Director: Even serious things?

Friend: Yes. Don't you agree?

Director: I don't know. What if you had a great many serious things to try and take lightly?

Friend: That would be my test.

Director: And if you can maintain your humor, you've held to your destiny?

Friend: Yes.

Director: But wouldn't some people say that a true comic destiny is filled with light things rather than the serious?

Friend: Well, that would be all the better.

Director: But then there wouldn't be the test you mentioned. So tell me. Do you believe destiny always involves a test?

Friend: I do.

Director: Then what's the test for those whose lives are filled with light things?

Friend: Not to get carried away.

Director: What keeps you from getting carried away?

Friend: Awareness.

Director: Of what?

Friend: Of just how lucky you are.

AMBITION (ARTIST)

Artist: An ambitious character has to believe in destiny.

Director: Why?

Artist: Because what drive to succeed is there if not for that?

Director: I'm not sure I understand. Can't you want something very badly without believing it's your destiny to obtain it?

Artist: Yes.

Director: And couldn't you be driven by your desire?

Artist: Yes, yes. But what happens when you run into trouble?

Director: I don't know. What happens?

Artist: You have to believe you'll get through it. And why do you believe? Because it's your destiny to get through.

Director: But why do you have to believe you'll get through it? Why can't you just try your best and hope you'll get through?

Artist: You act as though you've never had to get through anything hard.

Director: Well, what do you, you yourself, do when you run into trouble?

Artist: I do what you said.

Director: What? You just try your best and hope?

Artist: Of course. But I'm not an ambitious character. So I don't have to believe.

Director: I don't know how seriously to take you. So tell me. What's the difference between hope and belief?

Artist: Hope involves the heart. Belief involves the soul.

Director: But, Artist, what do you say to those who think heart and soul can and should be one?

Artist: I say, good luck.

MONEY (SCIENTIST)

Scientist: Science can't proceed without financial support.

Director: Why not?

Scientist: Because science is dependent on technology.

Director: Isn't that putting the cart before the horse?

Scientist: Yes, I know what you mean. But how can we do without new means of observation, new means of measurement, and so on?

Director: Is that how the great discoveries come? Through these new means?

Scientist: Often enough? Yes.

Director: So, technology is expensive. And that makes financial support critical. But is science destined to always have the financial support it needs, or deserves?

Scientist: That depends on whether people keep believing in it.

Director: What makes them believe?

Scientist: Benefits. Real, tangible benefits.

Director: And without them the money dries up?

Scientist: Oh, there will always be some money. There are those who believe in pure science, bless them. But yes, the money dries up without benefits.

Director: So science operates at three removes.

Scientist: What do you mean?

Director: Science needs technology. Technology needs money. Money needs benefits.

Scientist: True.

Director: What would it take for science to operate directly, at no remove?

Scientist: We'd have to put the horse back in front of the cart.

Director: And?

Scientist: More people would have to develop a taste, a hunger — for truth.

Deserving (Friend)

Friend: Do good destinies go to the deserving?

Director: Honestly? I don't know.

Friend: Why not?

Director: Because I don't know what we mean by 'good'.

Friend: What do you think we mean?

Director: Fitting.

Friend: A good destiny is a fitting destiny?

Director: Wouldn't you agree?

Friend: Yes, I suppose I would. But then do you know what that means?

Director: Tell me.

Friend: It means you always deserve a good destiny because your destiny should always fit.

Director: Yes. But let's be clear. If you're bad, what's a fitting destiny?

Friend: A bad destiny.

Director: But what does 'bad' mean?

Friend: Ha, ha, ha.

Director: Why do you laugh?

Friend: Because you want me to say it's the opposite of good!

Director: Is it?

Friend: Yes, of course! So 'bad' would be something that's the opposite of fitting.

Director: I agree.

Friend: But then we have to say that an ill fitting destiny for someone who's bad is good!

Director: Which means it fits? Well, then the bad get exactly what they deserve.

Honor (Artist)

Artist: How would I portray honor? Well, it depends.

Director: On what?

Artist: On which type of honor you mean.

Director: I didn't know there's more than one type of honor.

Artist: Director, where have you been? Of course there is.

Director: What types have you got in mind?

Artist: The first is the honor you get from others. The second is the honor you get from yourself.

Director: You mean you honor yourself?

Artist: Yes, and one who does that is always the more interesting character to portray.

Director: Why?

Artist: Because that character will always have the harder time.

Director: But why?

Artist: Don't pretend you don't know. People can't stand when people honor themselves.

Director: They think the self-honoring think they're better?

Artist: Yes.

Director: But are they better?

Artist: Between you and me? They are.

Director: Then I think you should always portray this type of character.

Artist: As a lesson to those who don't honor themselves?

Director: Not so much that. I was thinking more that you'd provide encouragement to those who do. Because, as you said, they'll have the harder time. But if through your art you can provide them with a taste of what their ultimate destiny might be...

Artist: ...they might be all the more willing to live it. Yes.

ANOTHER LIFE (SCIENTIST)

Scientist: Science is concerned with this life.

Director: Unless it finds evidence of another life?

Scientist: True evidence? Then that other life would also become the concern of science.

Director: But let's be sure what we're talking about. The afterlife?

Scientist: Yes, of course. Or a parallel life. Or rebirth. And so on.

Director: Let's stick with the afterlife. If science can penetrate there, will it explore it as an uncharted world?

Scientist: Yes — and with zeal!

Director: So what would this mean for our destiny?

Scientist: I don't know. What do you think it would mean?

Director: Well, tell me. Where do you think our ultimate destiny lies?

Scientist: As in this world or the next? I don't think we know enough to say.

Director: Let's suppose our destiny leads us into an afterlife and there it rests.

Scientist: The afterlife is the end point of our destiny? I think that's what many people believe.

Director: Then what happens to people who don't live out their destiny in this world?

Scientist: Their destiny is incomplete when they reach the other world? Then they might have no end point in the afterlife. No closure. And they might be compelled to live out their remaining destiny over the course of eternity, or however long the afterlife lasts. And that would be bitter or sweet depending on whether their remaining destiny is bad or good.

Director: So there's no escaping destiny?

Scientist: Not if we assume such an afterlife, no. But even if we don't I don't think we should try to escape.

Director: Then let's live up to it now — and leave ourselves free for whatever may come.

Hidden (Friend)

Friend: Do you think people's destiny can be hidden?

Director: I think it's possible for people's destiny to be hidden both from themselves and from others.

Friend: Do you think that's bad?

Director: I don't know. It might not be good for certain others to know your destiny, at least in its early stages. They might try to get in the way.

Friend: But what about being hidden from yourself?

Director: Well, what if you need to grow more as a person before you're prepared to accept your destiny and act on it — and the universe knows this and hides your destiny from you?

Friend: A good point. But I wonder what you think about this. What if you live your life without knowing your destiny — while actually walking with destiny all the while?

Director: You want to know if that's better than not living your destiny? I suppose it is. But it's better still to know your destiny, too.

Friend: Yes, of course. But tell me what knowing it brings.

Director: For many? Confidence and satisfaction. Those two, I think.

Friend: I think you're right. So how do we unhide the hidden?

Director: If your hypothetical holds, where you live your destiny without knowing it? Others will surely see your destiny taking shape.

Friend: And I can learn about my destiny from them? But you know I'm uneasy about that. Wouldn't it be better to learn about it on my own?

Director: If you can see yourself objectively? Sure, that would be great. But so long as you learn, truly learn — does it really matter much how?

Friend: But if I learn from others, wouldn't it be better if I could learn both from them and myself? That way I could verify what they say.

Director: Of course you have to verify what others say. Their words are simple prompts for you to be honest with yourself — and to uncover whatever you have inside.

Enemies (Artist)

Artist: Good enemies make for a good destiny.

Director: Provided you overcome them?

Artist: Not necessarily. Don't you know it can be good to put up a good fight and lose?

Director: So it's a good fight that makes for a good destiny, win or lose. But what makes for a good fight?

Artist: Fighting against long odds. Standing up to a terrible foe. You know.

Director: Then a good enemy is a terrible enemy with the odds on its side. But do our heroes love their good enemies?

Artist: Why would they?

Director: For giving them the chance to have a good destiny.

Artist: Yes, yes. But they hate their enemies.

Director: Then is that part of their destiny? To be torn between love and hate?

Artist: No, I wouldn't say they're torn — because what they love most about their enemies is to destroy them!

Director: I take your point. But tell me, Artist. Is there any way to have a good destiny without good enemies?

Artist: If you have weak enemies? Or indifferent enemies? Or no enemies at all? No. There's no good destiny in that.

Director: Destiny aside, would you say we can judge people by their enemies?

Artist: I would. And who do you think my enemies are?

Director: All those who oppose the meaning of your work. Who else?

Artist: Ha! My meaning....

Director: Why do you say it like that?

Artist: Because all who fail to grasp my meaning oppose it, whether they know it or not. And the odds are, to put it mildly, on their side. But are they terrible? I'll let you tell me.

Random (Scientist)

Scientist: Does anything random happen in the universe or is it all destined or fated to be? Why would you ask that, Director?

Director: Because science seeks the causes of all things. And if we know the cause of something, we know it's not random. No?

Scientist: Well, it's true. The random is only where we don't yet know the cause. Randomness is a sort of excuse for our lack of knowledge.

Director: Then let me ask you the hard question.

Scientist: By all means.

Director: How does this apply to human beings?

Scientist: Ah, you're wondering once again about free will and choice, meaningful choice.

Director: Well?

Scientist: Some would say we have no choice. That we're determined in all we do.

Director: What would you say?

Scientist: I believe in free will.

Director: Do you mean that you believe we're free to do random things?

Scientist: It's funny when you put it that way — but yes. And yes, I understand the implication. We can do random things because we don't yet know what causes us to do these things. But what about you?

Director: I'm inclined to say that we have only one true choice.

Scientist: Oh? What choice is that?

Director: What we choose to believe.

Scientist: Interesting! We believe when we don't know. And that's exactly what we do when it comes to randomness. We believe what we're seeing is random when in fact it's almost certainly not. But tell me. Do you think some beliefs are random?

Director: For some? Who can say? But for others? I think we can know the cause.

In Your Eyes (Friend)

Friend: Can you see destiny in the eyes of another?

Director: Yes, but I think there are two senses to this.

Friend: What are they?

Director: One, you can see that the other walks with destiny. Two, you can see your own destiny reflected.

Friend: Can you see you have a destiny together?

Director: Yes, I suppose you can, Friend. But that's harder to see.

Friend: Why?

Director: Because doesn't it presuppose you're able to see both the other's destiny and your own before you can see the two of them together?

Friend: I don't agree. I think sometimes you can see you have a destiny together even though you don't know the individual destinies.

Director: Hmm. Tell me. Assuming you know your destiny together as well as your individual destinies — which is stronger? Your combined destiny or that of each of you alone?

Friend: I don't think there can be any doubt. Your destiny together is always stronger.

Director: Why is that?

Friend: Because it's always harder to break two sticks that are bound together than one alone.

Director: So any stick will do for strength?

Friend: Of course not.

Director: You must mean you want a strong stick, not one that's rotten.

Friend: Yes. But strength isn't everything. You need some suppleness, too.

Director: And what about the beauty of the wood?

Friend: Why, Director, beauty is the very thing that keeps the two sticks bound.

A God (Artist)

Artist: I am the god of my works.

Director: I congratulate you.

Artist: I define the destinies of each and every character.

Director: You are a mighty god.

Artist: But do you know what's the hardest part of all?

Director: Insufficient worship?

Artist: No! The hardest part is that when my works are at their best, my hand, the hand of fate — is invisible. Do you have any idea how hard it is to be invisible?

Director: I'm afraid I've never played the role of god.

Artist: Well, I can tell you. It isn't easy. Everything in the vain artist's blood wants to scream out, Look at me! Look at me!

Director: But you resist?

Artist: I bury those feelings deep down inside.

Director: Bury them where?

Artist: In my subconscious, of course.

Director: But if you know what's in your subconscious, can it really be subconscious?

Artist: Of course it can! I'm a creative god. Who can say what happens with me?

Director: Okay. But why bury your feelings at all? Why not keep them firmly in mind?

Artist: Because they would be a distraction. And here's the problem. Vain feelings birth vain thoughts which birth vain works of art.

Director: Hmm. Maybe you can work on having more modest feelings?

Artist: Yes, yes. But modest feelings birth modest thoughts which birth modest works.

Director: Then decide on the type of work you want and shape your feelings accordingly. Surely a god of your prowess can do as much as this.

Collaboration (Scientist)

Scientist: How is true scientific collaboration possible if everyone is focused on their individual destinies and not on the overarching goal?

Director: But don't the individual destinies of scientists all point to that goal?

Scientist: You would think they would, but that's not always the case. Some people are more worried about making a name for themselves than working together disinterestedly.

Director: But if they work together and achieve the goal, won't they have made a name for themselves? They wouldn't be the only name, but a name nonetheless. No?

Scientist: Yes, of course. But sometimes pride and ego get in the way and drive collaborating scientists apart.

Director: Well, that's a shame. What's to do be done?

Scientist: If you're the lead scientist, you only take on others who put science first.

Director: Ahead of destiny?

Scientist: Science should be their destiny.

Director: How would you be able to tell if is?

Scientist: They would have to be wholly, completely, dedicated to the cause.

Director: The cause of your project?

Scientist: No, of course not. The cause of science.

Director: But you would want them to be dedicated to your project. No?

Scientist: Yes, and the only way it all works is if my project itself wholly serves science's cause.

Director: Which means you allow nothing to get in the way of science, pure and true.

Scientist: Precisely.

Director: Well, it all sounds very simple.

Scientist: And, oh, how rarely it is.

High Office (Friend)

Friend: Do those who obtain to high office always believe it's their destiny?

Director: No, I don't think all of them do.

Friend: Which kind of officials would you want serving you?

Director: The most able.

Friend: Regardless of the beliefs they hold about themselves?

Director: No, I wouldn't say that.

Friend: Then what would you say?

Director: That their beliefs shouldn't get in the way of their doing their job.

Friend: But what if the job gets in the way of their beliefs?

Director: I suppose they have three choices. They can resign, they can change their beliefs, or they can work to change the job.

Friend: Tailor the job to their destiny?

Director: Yes.

Friend: But changing the job is hard.

Director: Holding high office is hard.

Friend: But won't people object?

Director: People will object to everything those in high office do. So why not do this?

Friend: Are you more effective a leader if the job suits your destiny?

Director: Destiny is a force. Don't you think it's best for leaders to put that force to work?

Friend: But can they do so openly?

Director: Make their destiny known? Ah, that's rarely possible.

Friend: Why?

Director: The fact that you raised the question, my friend, suggests that you know why.

TRUE LOVE (ARTIST)

Artist: Do those who find true love always believe it's destiny?

Director: So, you're working on something to do with love?

Artist: Yes. Now tell me what you think.

Director: 'Always' is such a hard word.

Artist: Oh, great. You're going to say, 'Sometimes they believe it's destiny and sometimes not.' Well?

Director: But it's true!

Artist: Okay. But who are the people who believe one way or the other?

Director: You're looking for types?

Artist: Yes. One type of person is destined to believe. Another is destined not to believe. So say it.

Director: But I don't know the types.

Artist: Liar! Of course you do. You, if anyone, know.

Director: Then I'll say that the modest believe true love is destiny.

Artist: Very good. And what about those who don't think it's destiny? Who are they?

Director: The proud.

Artist: Why don't they believe?

Director: They believe in something else. They believe it's only just they found their love.

Artist: Well, modesty and destiny; pride and justice. You may be on to something here.

Director: Maybe. But can't you see the problem? We can switch it around. Modesty goes with justice as well as pride goes with destiny. So who's to say?

Artist: Not you, it seems. But let's work it through. I can see how the proud might believe their love came through either justice or destiny. And I can see how the modest might believe the same. But I'm inclined to say that both of them are wrong on every count. True love in truth is just blind luck. And knowing that deep inside drives every lover mad.

An Idea (Scientist)

Scientist: Not all success is great. And not all greatness is successful.

Director: So which would you rather be?

Scientist: Great, of course.

Director: Even at the cost of success?

Scientist: Some of the greatest men and women in the world were failures in their day.

Director: So you're more interested in posthumous success?

Scientist: No, don't get me wrong. I'm as interested as anyone in success during my life. But if it's a question of sacrificing greatness in order to achieve it, then no thanks.

Director: What destines someone to be great?

Scientist: An idea.

Director: Can you say more?

Scientist: Dedication to an idea, come hell or high water.

Director: Can this idea be wrong?

Scientist: It's funny you should ask. Yes, I suppose it can.

Director: But you want an idea that's right.

Scientist: Of course I do.

Director: And for the right idea to succeed, what does it take?

Scientist: Critical mass.

Director: You mean enough people believing in it?

Scientist: Precisely.

Director: And sometimes that comes during your life, and sometimes after?

Scientist: That's right. So all you can do is promote your idea with all your might and hope it catches on. And if it does, there's a good chance you'll be... remembered.

In Support (Friend)

Friend: What if your destiny in life is to play a supporting role? Some people can't accept that, even though it might make them happy.

Director: Why do you think they might not be able to accept such a role?

Friend: Because everyone seems to want to be the star.

Director: And if you're less than the star you've failed?

Friend: That's what they think.

Director: Then tell me. What does it mean to be a star?

Friend: To stand out. To shine.

Director: For all too see?

Friend: Of course.

Director: Do you imagine it's always pleasant for 'all to see'?

Friend: No, I can imagine that creates a lot of pressure.

Director: But there's less pressure in being in a supporting role?

Friend: Less pressure from 'all' but more from the star, who might lean too much on you.

Director: What if you were blessed with a good star?

Friend: You mean one who knows how much to lean?

Director: Yes.

Friend: Then being in a supporting role might not be so bad.

Director: Might not be so bad? Or might be pretty good?

Friend: Might be pretty good.

Director: Then we should hunt for stars like this.

Friend: And if we find ourselves to be the star?

Director: Well, then we'll know what we need to do.

Madness (Artist)

Artist: Tell me, Director. What destines you to go mad?

Director: Oh, Artist, I really don't know.

Artist: Sure you do! Come on. I need your input. My next work deals with madness.

Director: Alright. I'll offer a suggestion. Take your characters and show them torn all their lives between two opposing things, both compelling.

Artist: And that would be enough to drive them mad?

Director: No, there's more. Have them fail to choose — and lose them both.

Artist: Ah yes, and then they'll despair. And that would do it?

Director: That's my best guess. What do you think?

Artist: I think there's more. I'll have to heap on the suffering, beyond being torn.

Director: Yes, that's probably a good idea.

Artist: So it's feeling torn, suffering greatly, and succumbing to despair. That's what drives my characters mad.

Director: Yes. Unless....

Artist: Unless what?

Director: Unless it's just a chemical thing.

Artist: No, it can never be that.

Director: Why not?

Artist: It's too boring! There's no story if madness is just a chemical thing.

Director: So what stance do you have to take?

Artist: I must show that any chemical imbalance comes as a result of these other things — the feeling torn, the suffering, and so on.

Director: But does correcting the imbalance free them of all that?

Artist: Ha! Not for my characters. Who am I to offer them an easy way out?

Clever (Scientist)

Scientist: Do the clever have better destinies? I suppose it depends on what use they put their cleverness to.

Director: But can we really say you're clever if you put your cleverness to bad use? Is it clever to do that? Or is it something else, something cunning, or crafty, and so on?

Scientist: I think you have a point.

Director: So the clever by definition put their cleverness to good use.

Scientist: Let's say they do.

Director: Then the question is whether good use leads to a better destiny.

Scientist: Yes.

Director: Why wouldn't it?

Scientist: Because destiny might be destiny and there's nothing we can do.

Director: True. But, on the other hand, there might be something we can do. Yes?

Scientist: Agreed.

Director: So how would we proceed, assuming there's something we can do?

Scientist: We'd use our cleverness not just to influence our own individual destinies for the better. We'd use it to influence all of our destinies for the better. I think that's the best thing we can do.

Director: So the more influence we have in the world for the better, the better?

Scientist: Right.

Director: Then answer this. What if you could influence the world to have a better destiny, but doing so makes for a rotten destiny for you? Would you do it?

Scientist: But how is that even possible? You would have a great destiny!

Director: Would it be great if the world were ungrateful and mistreated you?

Scientist: Yes, though it would be better if you were clever enough to avoid all that.

Intrigue (Friend)

Friend: Can your destiny be good if you involve yourself in intrigue?

Director: I suppose it depends on the intrigue. Have you got a particular kind in mind?

Friend: Yes. Say we live in a tyranny, and we secretly plot to overthrow the tyrant in order to be free.

Director: And you want to know if it's possible to have a good destiny, regardless of whether we succeed?

Friend: Yes, succeed or fail. The question is about the attempt itself. So what do you think?

Director: Hmm. I think the question turns on whether the intrigue is necessary or not.

Friend: If this intrigue isn't necessary, I don't know what is! So our destiny is good. Yes?

Director: Let's say it is, even if we fail — because we'll live on as examples of resistance. But now let's consider another example — intrigue when it comes to love.

Friend: That's not necessary intrigue. And so that can never be good.

Director: That was my first impression, too. But then I got to thinking. Have you ever heard it said that love can be a tyrant?

Friend: Sure, but that's just a figure of speech.

Director: But aren't there reasons why we use particular figures of speech?

Friend: True. So what point are you trying to make?

Director: That it's necessary to overthrow love when it becomes tyrannical.

Friend: Either in yourself or the other? But why intrigue? Why not just walk away?

Director: Sometimes, if things have gotten bad enough, it takes intrigue just to walk away. Can't you imagine all kinds of dependencies, emotional and otherwise, that grow up in a situation involving tyrannical love? To break through them all, sometimes we have to make secret plans for escape.

Friend: That makes sense. So our destiny would be good here, too?

Director: Yes. But only if we succeed.

Friends (Artist)

Artist: If you were destined to do nothing but have good friends, would you be happy?

Director: Yes, I imagine I would. How about you?

Artist: I wouldn't be happy.

Director: Why not?

Artist: Because I'd need my work.

Director: Would you share your works with friends?

Artist: Yes, of course.

Director: And that would make them better friends?

Artist: I think it would.

Director: Then your art serves the cause of friendship.

Artist: True. But what about you? What do you bring to our table of friends? Philosophy?

Director: Do you see anything wrong with that?

Artist: No, I don't. In fact, I think philosophy is an art of sorts.

Director: An art which will make me have better friends?

Artist: Yes.

Director: Just how exactly do our arts make us have better friends?

Artist: Exactly? Oh, come on, Director! Who can say these things?

Director: We can, friend.

Artist: Ha! Alright. Let's take ourselves as examples. My art and your philosophy give us something to talk about.

Director: And that's the most important thing for friends? But can't you have plenty to talk about with those who strictly speaking aren't your friends?

Artist: Yes, yes. But it's sweeter to talk with friends. In fact, it's that sweetness in conversation that lets you know you've found a friend. So talk, and taste — and see.

EARNING (SCIENTIST)

Scientist: No worthwhile destiny comes without obstacles.

Director: What's wrong with a destiny without obstacles?

Scientist: You haven't earned anything.

Director: And that's what makes a destiny worthwhile? Earning it? So what do you think about this as a metaphor for destiny? On the one hand, I might save my money to buy a house. On the other hand, I might inherit the same house from a relative. Isn't the house the house, no matter how obtained?

Scientist: Yes, but which way would make you feel better?

Director: Are you asking if I'd feel proud for having bought the house?

Scientist: I am. And wouldn't you?

Director: It seems to me I might feel proud either way.

Scientist: Why? On the one hand you used your hard earned money and bought the house. On the other hand it was simply given to you.

Director: Yes, but can't we say I earned the inheritance by being loyal and kind to my relative for a very long time?

Scientist: Yes, but it's not the same thing.

Director: What if the relative were a particularly difficult person, always throwing up obstacles to having good relations? Would I have earned it then?

Scientist: Well... I think we've somehow gotten off track.

Director: How so? We're saying a worthwhile destiny comes with obstacles. Right? And I'm saying an inherited destiny might involve obstacles, significant obstacles.

Scientist: But do you really want your destiny at second hand?

Director: Ah, that's what's troubling you. Well, tell me. Is a destiny second hand if you manage to make it your own? Wouldn't it take a complete renovation, as it were, to make it truly yours, as much so as if you'd had it built new? You'd have to work very hard to accomplish that, assuming you do it yourself. And if you do, who are we to say you haven't earned your destiny — and a healthy bit of pride?

Drowning (Friend)

Friend: Have you ever heard people say they're drowning?

Director: Yes, I have. What do you think they mean?

Friend: That they have too many things to deal with all at once. So here's what I want to know. Can you be on your way to destiny if you're drowning?

Director: You're talking about for more than brief moments here and there?

Friend: Yes, I'm talking about all the time.

Director: Then no. I don't think you can be on your way.

Friend: In that case, what can you do?

Director: Learn to swim.

Friend: And what does learning to swim mean?

Director: Focusing on the most important things and doing them well.

Friend: But what if everything seems important?

Director: Equally important?

Friend: Yes. Don't you think that's possible?

Director: No, I don't.

Friend: What? Really?

Director: Really.

Friend: But how will you know what's most important?

Director: By coming to see your destiny more clearly.

Friend: I don't understand.

Director: What's most important is what supports your destiny best.

Friend: But isn't that selfish?

Director: Yes. But are you forgetting? The alternative is to drown.

Faithless (Artist)

Artist: Can you have a good destiny if you're faithless? It depends what we mean by 'good'.

Director: Oh, I would have thought it depends on what we mean by 'faith'.

Artist: Well, tell me what you think 'faith' means.

Director: Let me give you an example. I have faith in you as a friend.

Artist: But what does that mean?

Director: For one, it means I trust you.

Artist: What else does it mean?

Director: That I believe you're going to fully become yourself.

Artist: And what on earth does that mean?

Director: That you will live your destiny to the full.

Artist: But I don't have a destiny. So what good is your faith?

Director: Well, maybe it's misplaced.

Artist: Yes. So let's get back to our initial question. And now that you've offered a somewhat off point definition of 'faith', why don't we change it around? Let's ask: Can your destiny be good if no one has faith in you?

Director: I think it's a terrible thing if no one has faith in you. But I think it can also be hard when others do have faith.

Artist: Why?

Director: Because if it's true that you know your destiny best, the faith of others, though largely correct about you, can be a source of confusion.

Artist: You mean my destiny might be BCDEF, but someone who has faith in me might think it's ABCDE, or something like that?

Director: Yes. So enjoy the faith of others. It's truly a gift. But be wary. And stay close to what you know you need to be, what you truly are. And then I'd say your destiny just might be good.

GOOD AND BAD (SCIENTIST)

Scientist: Do the moral have good destinies while the immoral have bad destinies?

Director: I'd change the question. I'd drop 'good' and 'bad' and leave us with this: Do the moral have destinies while the immoral don't?

Scientist: But why do you want the question to be this?

Director: Because it might more accurately reflect the truth.

Scientist: How so?

Director: Destiny might be beyond good and bad.

Scientist: Beyond good and bad? You mean destiny just... is?

Director: That's how it sometimes seems to me.

Scientist: Is that because there are some good and bad things about every destiny?

Director: Yes. And no matter how many the good or the bad, destiny is destiny. No?

Scientist: It is. But that still doesn't get at our question, our revised question about having a destiny or not.

Director: Well, what's your opinion?

Scientist: I'm finding it hard to have an opinion. If we say that only the moral have destinies, I very much want to add: And those destinies are good! But you're asking me to resist doing just that. So what do you think?

Director: Shouldn't we keep it simple? Yes, the moral have destinies. No, the immoral don't.

Scientist: But there's a problem with that. What about infamous villains? No destiny?

Director: I'd say no. After all, aren't infamy and destiny two very different things?

Scientist: I suppose they are. But that means fame and destiny are also two very different things.

Director: That's true. And the sooner more people come to see that, the better off I think we'll all be.

JUSTICE (FRIEND)

Friend: Is destiny just?

Director: In what sense?

Friend: In the sense of giving us what we deserve.

Director: Who's to say what we deserve?

Friend: Don't you think there's a general consensus?

Director: I do. But I wouldn't say it's always right.

Friend: But then you admit you have a standard for what we deserve. You call it 'right'.

Director: It's hard not to have such a standard, wouldn't you say?

Friend: I think it's impossible to live in this world and not have a standard for this.

Director: Well, let me ask you. Have you ever felt that someone didn't get the destiny that he or she deserved?

Friend: Of course. It happens all the time. The deserving don't always get justice.

Director: Then it seems there are two possibilities here. One, we're wrong about what these people deserve. Or two, we're right but the world itself is unjust. Which seems more likely to you?

Friend: You want me to say it's more likely we're wrong. But I think we're right. And the world is unjust.

Director: So where does that leave us?

Friend: It leaves us fighting a fight that's all but impossible to win.

Director: Then what does that make us? Crazy or brave?

Friend: You know I think it makes us brave.

Director: Yes, but don't discount the crazy.

Friend: Why?

Director: Because sometimes crazy is what it takes to win.

Power (Artist)

Artist: Is power more of a help or a hindrance to reaching your destiny? The question is ridiculous. Power is always a help — for everything!

Director: But what kind of power are you talking about?

Artist: Any kind of power. Physical power. Mental power. Financial power. Political power. And so on, and so on.

Director: But what if you don't know how to use your power?

Artist: Then you can't very well travel your way.

Director: So power isn't always a help. But what about the other way? What if you know how to use power but don't have any?

Artist: Really, Director. How can you know how to use power without having it?

Director: You need to have it in order to learn how to use it?

Artist: Yes, of course. Or do you think you can just read a book about how to use power and that's enough?

Director: But isn't that dangerous? I mean do we want someone to have great power and not know how to use it properly, at least for a time?

Artist: It happens every day, regardless of whether we like it or not.

Director: I suppose you have a point. But there's one power you mentioned that I'm wondering about in particular now. The power of the mind. Can we not know how to use our minds?

Artist: There's no doubt about that. Many people don't know how to use the power of their minds. And when they don't, they can't know how to use any other power, either.

Director: But what if we use a mere fraction of our minds in order to learn how to use a particular power, and we don't know how to use the rest?

Artist: Then the rest of the mind rots. It's like all power. If you don't use it, you lose it.

Director: Then let's be sure to use it. And let's encourage everyone we know to use it!

Artist: Ah, sometimes you seem so charmingly naive.

Prayer (Scientist)

Scientist: What harm could there be in praying to obtain your destiny?

Director: You might pray and just leave it to God, doing nothing to obtain it yourself. And in that case I would say there's a definite harm.

Scientist: Yes, that's true. But do you think it's ever wise to pray?

Director: I don't know if you'll like what I have to say.

Scientist: Oh, don't worry about me. Nothing surprises me anymore when it comes to these things.

Director: Then I'll tell you. Prayer seems wise when it strengthens your resolve to live your fate.

Scientist: But why did you think I wouldn't like that?

Director: Isn't it obvious?

Scientist: Not to me.

Director: I didn't think you'd like it because we all know there are other ways to strengthen your resolve.

Scientist: And this means prayer can be replaced?

Director: Do you think it can?

Scientist: No, because it might be necessary for one important thing.

Director: What thing?

Scientist: Finding our way. We often pray to God for that.

Director: But how do we come to know our way? Through signs? Twelve eagles in the sky, a thunderbolt out of the blue, a tree that bursts into flames?

Scientist: The signs don't have to be that dramatic. But when they're not, interpreting them can be hard. You see, there's a risk we'll force our will upon the signs and not see them for what they are. But then again sometimes a little will can do you good. After all, it's as you said — you can't just pray and leave it to God. You have to do most of the work yourself.

Easy (Friend)

Friend: Can living out your destiny be easy?

Director: For some people? I suppose so. They go with the flow.

Friend: That can be a destiny? Going with the flow?

Director: Why not? And what's easier than that?

Friend: There's nothing easier than that.

Director: Not even believing in a fixed idea?

Friend: What are you talking about?

Director: What's easier than being a stick in the mud that resists the flow?

Friend: Nothing, I suppose. You don't have to do anything but stay stuck.

Director: But what about those who go with the flow?

Friend: When you go with the flow you have to go where, well, the flow goes.

Director: Can that ever be difficult?

Friend: Now that I think of it, yes. There might be rapids and tricky waters ahead.

Director: But sticks in the mud?

Friend: They're always just where they are.

Director: Which is to say they never go anywhere. Or have we got it wrong?

Friend: No, I think we're making an excellent point. And here's something I've noticed. The sticks in the mud tend to think they're morally superior.

Director: For being stuck in the mud?

Friend: Exactly.

Director: Would it be better for them to get unstuck?

Friend: Yes. But what do they do then?

Director: Get out of the flow and onto dry land — and go wherever they please.

Déja Vu (Artist)

Artist: Oh, I employ déja vu all the time. It means you're walking with destiny, that you're on the right path.

Director: Just because you think you've seen something before?

Artist: Yes, definitely. It's a sign!

Director: Your art deals in signs?

Artist: Of course. I'm the one who creates the signs. And I interpret them.

Director: So you don't rely on fortune tellers and the like?

Artist: Bah! I steer well clear of them.

Director: Why?

Artist: Because they're bad luck — and they're generally wrong. I mean, tell a fortune teller you saw a three-eyed black crow thrice, and what do you think you'll get?

Director: I have no idea.

Artist: And neither does the fortune teller! Ha, ha, ha! But I can tell you what it means.

Director: So long as it's within the world you create?

Artist: And what's more real than that? But you must admit — only fools ignore déja vu.

Director: But I ignore it all the time.

Artist: Ah, Director. That will bring you the worst possible luck!

Director: Why?

Artist: Destiny knocks through déja vu — and wants you to answer the door!

Director: But what does that mean? It wants me to believe? But believe in what?

Artist: That there's more to life than we can possibly know.

Director: And what kind of faith is that?

Artist: The kind that kills science, my friend — as I'm sure you very well know.

Serendipity (Scientist)

Scientist: Happy accidents are signs that you walk with destiny.

Director: And unhappy accidents are signs that you don't?

Scientist: Yes.

Director: Hmm. Why do you think that is?

Scientist: Because those happy accidents are the universe's way of telling you to keep on your way.

Director: And it's just the opposite with unhappy accidents?

Scientist: It is. And, oh, don't think that I think everything is perfect when you're walking with destiny. It's not. But happy accidents ought to be treated as signs.

Director: But then are they really accidents? I mean, if the universe is encouraging us, is giving us signs — can that be chance?

Scientist: Well, you have a point. So let's say it isn't chance. It's destiny.

Director: I don't know about all this, Scientist.

Scientist: What don't you know?

Director: Are we saying that only those who walk with destiny have good luck?

Scientist: No, but there's a certain tendency over time.

Director: So those who walk their way tend to have better luck.

Scientist: Yes.

Director: Why do you think that is?

Scientist: When you're going where you need to go, you see the things you need to see.

Director: And when we see a thing we need to see, we take that as a happy sign?

Scientist: Of course. And if you're not where you need to be, if you're not on your way, you won't see the things you need to see, the things that belong to you, the things that are properly yours. But when you go to where you need to be, you have all that — and that's what I call serendipity.

CALM (FRIEND)

Friend: When you meet someone with a great sense of calm you know he or she is walking with destiny.

Director: Yes, I've often thought that. But can we be sure?

Friend: What do you mean?

Director: I mean what if a crisis unfolds and he or she just stays calm?

Friend: Isn't it best to be calm in a crisis?

Director: Yes. But what if there's a need for urgent action?

Friend: You stay calm while acting urgently.

Director: And if you don't act urgently but just remain calm?

Friend: I suppose you've stepped off the path of destiny.

Director: So tell me. What do you think it is that keeps someone on the path?

Friend: What makes them stay calm and act? I don't know.

Director: Well, what makes them stay calm?

Friend: Inner peace.

Director: And what makes for inner peace?

Friend: Knowing you're on your way.

Director: Can you be on your way and fail to act when a crisis comes?

Friend: Yes. Because there are other types of destiny than the heroic type.

Director: Is the heroic type quite rare?

Friend: Of course.

Director: And if rare deserving of praise?

Friend: The heroic deserve the highest praise we can give. And I think hope of that praise is what spurs many of them, but not the best, to act.

FAMILY (ARTIST)

Artist: Sure, family can be destiny.

Director: How so?

Artist: The family itself can have a destiny and you're a part of it.

Director: What if you don't want to be a part of it?

Artist: You have to break with it as I did long ago.

Director: Why didn't you want to be a part of that destiny?

Artist: Because my family is tyrannical.

Director: There's not just one tyrant in the family? The family itself, as a whole, is tyrannical?

Artist: That's right. They tried to force me into their destiny. And so I had to leave.

Director: Did your art help you break away?

Artist: It did. And now my art has an independent destiny.

Director: But would you say that other artists might well be part of a family destiny and still have an independent art?

Artist: Yes, yes — of course. It all depends on the family. No two are alike.

Director: So what would you say to artists living in a tyranny?

Artist: First, you must prove to yourself beyond a doubt that what you've got is tyranny.

Director: And how do you do that?

Artist: You test for signs of force concerning your art.

Director: Because your art resists the family will?

Artist: Yes. Tyrants can't stand when you resist. And if resistance — gentle resistance, tactful resistance — meets with force, over and over again? You know you have to leave.

Director: But if your family tolerates your work?

Artist: And your work is good? Then, Director, you're in the greatest possible luck.

Ideas (Scientist)

Scientist: Of course an idea can be our destiny.

Director: How so?

Scientist: We live up to it and it makes us what we are.

Director: What happens if we abandon the idea?

Scientist: Usually? We find another one to take its place.

Director: And if we don't?

Scientist: Well, here's the thing. Abandonment of an idea leaves a void, a vacuum.

Director: And something always rushes in to fill that void?

Scientist: Yes.

Director: But then why did you say we 'usually' find another idea? Shouldn't we say we 'always' find another idea?

Scientist: Voids can be filled with other things than ideas.

Director: Like what?

Scientist: Passions.

Director: Like love or hate?

Scientist: Of course.

Director: What's better to have? A good idea or love?

Scientist: It's best to have them both.

Director: And what's worse to have? A bad idea or hate? And this time you have to choose.

Scientist: I'd say, for the sake of others, it's better to have the bad idea.

Director: Why?

Scientist: Because your bad idea will often end with you alone.

Party (Friend)

Friend: Political parties have destinies just like families do.

Director: And your destiny is theirs to the extent you're attached?

Friend: Yes.

Director: But what if you feel you somehow belong yet have an independent destiny?

Friend: You can seek to shape the party.

Director: Steer it your way? But what if everyone is doing just that?

Friend: Then things get complicated.

Director: Yes, I'm sure they do. But, really, is 'everyone' the sort to take such initiative?

Friend: No, you have a point. Most people never take the initiative.

Director: And destiny belongs to those who do?

Friend: Right.

Director: Does this mean that those of initiative battle one another for control?

Friend: I suppose it does.

Director: What sort of person do you think wins? The nicest?

Friend: Definitely not.

Director: What sort then?

Friend: The most ruthless.

Director: Ruthless and dumb? Or ruthless and smart?

Friend: Smart, no doubt.

Director: Now, you're smart. And you can take initiative. Don't you lack just one thing?

Friend: Ruthlessness? But what if I say the party isn't my way?

Director: Then what will you do?

Friend: Take myself somewhere else — where the opposite of ruthlessness succeeds.

Conflict (Artist)

Artist: Good characters always have conflict in reaching their destiny.

Director: There's nothing exciting about people just strolling their way through?

Artist: Ha! A stroll in the park is nice for artists who have completed their labor of love. But for their characters? Excitement is the order of the day.

Director: And that excitement cuts both ways. I mean characters can win the conflict and they can lose. No?

Artist: Of course. But people don't like it when the good ones lose. They develop close emotional ties with these characters.

Director: Because they have their own conflict and are trying to reach their destiny, too?

Artist: Yes.

Director: So if you want to be popular, you'll have the characters people love succeed.

Artist: If I want to be popular.

Director: Don't you?

Artist: You know I scorn popularity. It's all too tied up with shallow souls.

Director: Oh, come on now, Artist. How can you know that? Who can say how deep or shallow someone is without getting to know them first?

Artist: Tell me, Director. Do you honestly believe there are more deep people than shallow in any given audience? Be honest, now. Tell me what you think.

Director: I think it's hard to say.

Artist: Ha! I think you're afraid to say. Well, I'll tell you. The shallow always outnumber the deep. And since I try to reach the deep, I have to get around the shallow somehow — and at times not be very popular along the way.

Director: That sounds like an excuse not to reach out to both shallow and deep.

Artist: Reach them both at once in the same work? Well, yes — that's possible. But the shallow and the deep would take away different things. And that, of course, is fine — assuming we don't mind their fighting it out over what it all means.

FLAWS (SCIENTIST)

Scientist: Of course a flawed person can have a good destiny. We're all flawed, after all, and some of us deserve good destinies.

Director: Yes. But tell me. Who among the flawed, the imperfect, deserves a bad destiny?

Scientist: Those with what we might call fatal flaws. For example, wanton disregard for others.

Director: And what's an example of a bad destiny that such a person deserves?

Scientist: Well, that's hard to say. I mean who am I to say exactly what someone else deserves? Suffice it to say it's bad.

Director: Okay. But now what about the other way around — a good destiny? Who deserves that? Those who have regard for others?

Scientist: Yes.

Director: Tell me. Can it ever be a flaw to have regard for others?

Scientist: Of course not.

Director: Then we can say with confidence that everyone should have regard for others?

Scientist: Yes, but you're only stating the obvious.

Director: Is it obvious that a soldier, for instance, should have regard for the enemy?

Scientist: Well, that doesn't quite sound right.

Director: Should the soldier disregard the enemy?

Scientist: No. The soldier needs to pay close attention to the enemy.

Director: So the soldier has regard, if only in a different sense?

Scientist: Yes, and you've made your point.

Director: Oh? What point is that?

Scientist: That context gives ambiguous words a different meaning.

Loyalty (Friend)

Friend: The loyal don't always have good destinies. I mean what if they're loyal to someone who's bad?

Director: Why would anyone be loyal to someone who's bad?

Friend: Because, Director, you're asked to be loyal before you know what someone's really like.

Director: If you wanted someone to become loyal to you, would you want them to get to know you first?

Friend: Definitely.

Director: So you'd expect the same of another who asks your loyalty?

Friend: That would only be fair, don't you think?

Director: I do. But even when you think you know someone, you might not. Isn't that true?

Friend: Of course it's true. You might be immature. You might lack perspective.

Director: So what if you've already pledged your loyalty to someone and then you mature, you gain perspective — and you don't like what you see with your new eyes?

Friend: Are you asking if you should become disloyal? I don't know. I can't see how that can be good.

Director: It's better to stay attached to someone who's bad?

Friend: Well, no, I suppose not. But what if it's not so clear a case?

Director: You mean the person is bad in some ways but not wholly?

Friend: Yes. What then?

Director: Can you just be loyal to the part that's good?

Friend: I think that would be hard.

Director: Why?

Friend: Because it would be obvious — and you might be asked to explain.

Violence (Artist)

Artist: Can people who use violence have good destinies? Yes.

Director: But are all of the violent good?

Artist: Of course not.

Director: What makes some of them good?

Artist: Well, we have to ask the questions — violent to whom, and why?

Director: But isn't one question sometimes enough?

Artist: What do you mean?

Director: If we answer 'violent to whom' and really tell who this person is, haven't we often suggested an answer to 'why'?

Artist: Ah, you're a clever one. Yes, that's true.

Director: So who deserves violence?

Artist: Those who trade in violence themselves.

Director: Violence begets violence?

Artist: Yes, and it all comes down to who used it first. What do you think?

Director: I wonder where it all ends.

Artist: Oh, you know as well as I — it never ends.

Director: If the violence never ends who can have a good destiny?

Artist: Those who are justified.

Director: Meaning they act in defense of themselves or others?

Artist: Of course.

Director: But is that enough?

Artist: You want to know if they must also prevail? Yes, yes — it's always best to be justified and prevail. And then the violence ends for a spell, which is really all we can hope.

Roles (Scientist)

Scientist: The roles we play in life certainly affect our destiny.

Director: Some would say just the right role is our destiny.

Scientist: Yes, that's true. That's why it's so important not to be stuck in a role we're not meant to play.

Director: How do we know when we're in such a role?

Scientist: Nothing goes right.

Director: Do you mean we're not successful?

Scientist: No, not quite that.

Director: Then what do you mean?

Scientist: I mean this. There's 'success' and then there's success.

Director: Are you saying we can be 'successful' in a role — but it's not truly our role?

Scientist: Yes.

Director: And it would be better to be 'unsuccessful' in a role that is our true role?

Scientist: Definitely.

Director: But can't the unsuccessful be rather unpleasant?

Scientist: Of course. It can be very unpleasant.

Director: Then it seems it's best both to be in our true role and to have success.

Scientist: Yes, and in that way success is success.

Director: How often do you think that happens?

Scientist: Success as success? I think it's rare.

Director: Because so many people are in the wrong role? But why do you think that is?

Scientist: Because they're dazzled by 'success'.

Director: Then may they find it — and learn that it's not what they think.

CHAPTERS (FRIEND)

Friend: If things look bad you can always start a new chapter in your life.

Director: How do you do that?

Friend: Turn the page and write something new.

Director: But what does it mean to turn the page?

Friend: It means you forget about the past.

Director: Is the past so easy to forget?

Friend: No, of course not. But it helps when you start writing something new.

Director: Because that's where your attention is?

Friend: Exactly.

Director: And if you keep on writing long enough? Does your new chapter come to alter the way you look at the old?

Friend: I don't know. Why do you think it might?

Director: Have you ever read a book and then gone back to the beginning and started all over again?

Friend: Of course.

Director: Didn't the beginning look different to you than it did the first time through?

Friend: It did. You can see more the second time round because of what you know happens later on.

Director: Yes. And why can't that be how it is with life?

Friend: Because in life we can't go back.

Director: Really? We can't look back and reflect?

Friend: Well, yes, of course. But what we see isn't always what was.

Director: But if we could truly see what was?

Friend: Then we'd have taken a further step down our way.

ACCIDENT (ARTIST)

Artist: There's always an element of accident to art.

Director: You mean in its creation?

Artist: Yes, but also within the work itself — the depiction of the accidental.

Director: I can understand how you'd say there must be accidents in the creation. But why would you say artists always depict the accidental? Couldn't an artist create something in which there is no accident?

Artist: Ha! Good luck with that. But even if it were possible, then art wouldn't mirror life.

Director: Because there's always the accidental in life?

Artist: Always.

Director: This mirroring is strange, though, isn't it? I mean, the deliberate creation of 'accident' is anything but accidental.

Artist: What can I say? Art is artificial.

Director: What would make it more natural, more like life?

Artist: Oh, letting the accidents attendant to the creation determine the work.

Director: Would such a natural process be better than one that's more artificial?

Artist: No, I don't think it would.

Director: Why?

Artist: Because it takes honest artifice to call attention to what the natural actually is.

Director: How is that done?

Artist: By condensing a great deal of interconnected accident into a very small space.

Director: Whereas nature's accidents are few and unconnected and far between?

Artist: You know better than that. They're many and connected and closely packed.

Director: Then why do we need art in order to see natural accident for what it is?

Artist: Because we hate to admit how accident dominates our lives.

Desire (Scientist)

Scientist: Are desires and destiny one?

Director: That's a question best posed to science.

Scientist: You think so? Why?

Director: Because science attempts to know all things, desires and destiny included. Or have I got it wrong?

Scientist: No. But then I think we need to narrow the question.

Director: What should we ask?

Scientist: If you follow your desires, do you live out your destiny?

Director: Is it the same if we ask: If you follow your heart, do you live out your destiny?

Scientist: Yes, I think it is.

Director: And what if we ask: If you follow your dreams, do you live out your destiny?

Scientist: I think it's all basically the same — dreams, heart, desires.

Director: And if science comes to know how all these things work and what they mean?

Scientist: Then destiny will be served much better than before.

Director: Really? Science would be willing to become an active agent in people's lives?

Scientist: Well, not science itself. Technology would facilitate this.

Director: Yes, how could I have forgotten? Science doesn't like to dirty its hands.

Scientist: You know that's not fair. To look objectively you always must get down into the dirt. Science isn't afraid to roll up its sleeves.

Director: Maybe when it's trying to learn. But after it's learned?

Scientist: You're asking if science loses interest?

Director: I am.

Scientist: That's not something I care to admit.

Company (Friend)

Friend: The company you keep certainly affects your destiny.

Director: Does good company make for a good destiny and bad company bad?

Friend: I have to say I think that's true.

Director: Then why would anyone ever keep bad company?

Friend: Maybe they're not strong enough to keep good company.

Director: Can you say more?

Friend: Good company maintains high standards. It takes strength to live up to high standards.

Director: So if you're weak you keep bad company, company with low standards?

Friend: Yes.

Director: Then we're saying something interesting.

Friend: What?

Director: We're saying the strong have good destinies and the weak bad.

Friend: That's not exactly what I meant.

Director: What did you mean?

Friend: I meant....

Director: What's wrong with saying the strong have good destinies?

Friend: You don't know? It's not fair!

Director: Not fair that some of us built up our strength and others didn't?

Friend: Well, when you put it like that....

Director: But even if we say it's not fair — does that make what we say about the weak and the strong any less true?

Friend: I think you have a point. Life isn't fair. But that doesn't mean we should ignore what's true. And so I'll say it again. Good company and good destiny go hand in hand.

Corruption (Artist)

Artist: Societies gradually, inevitably, become corrupt. The best that can be done is to slow the corruption down.

Director: And that's possible because not all people are corrupt, even in a bad society?

Artist: Yes, of course.

Director: What's it like to be destined to be honest in a worsening state?

Artist: Ah, that, my friend, makes for a good story.

Director: I agree. But you seem to be taking some sort of delight in the notion. Why?

Artist: Why? Ha! You can torture the protagonist in such a tale — and that only makes people believe in her or him even more!

Director: I always knew you had a sadistic streak.

Artist: Oh, come on! It's all for the good. I'd let the protagonist fight corruption and win.

Director: But would you prefer a different outcome?

Artist: Fight and lose? What are you saying, friend? There's no story in that. It happens every day.

Director: People stand up to corruption every day? Maybe we're not living on the same planet, my friend.

Artist: Yes, alright, alright. They don't stand up. But they resent corruption all the same.

Director: If you wanted to feed that resentment, then wouldn't you let your protagonist fight and lose?

Artist: No. You see, such a story might only serve to bring good people's spirits down.

Director: And when they're down they don't fight to slow corruption?

Artist: Yes. So if we're hoping for them to fight we'll let the hero win. That's how we inspire.

Director: But if society is largely corrupt, how many really want to be inspired?

Artist: There's an easy way to know. We'll simply judge from how much profit we take in.

INCORRUPTIBILITY (SCIENTIST)

Scientist: I love science because it's incorruptible.

Director: Don't scientists sometimes fake data?

Scientist: Well, yes. They do.

Director: And aren't there jealousies and bitter rivalries and so on?

Scientist: True.

Director: But aside from that sort of messy stuff, on the whole, science remains pristine?

Scientist: Yes.

Director: Would you say you have a belief in science? A faith?

Scientist: I trust in science as the only pure thing I know.

Director: And to the extent science has a destiny, you want that to be your destiny, too?

Scientist: I hitch my wagon to science, as they say.

Director: What makes science incorruptible?

Scientist: Truth can either be demonstrated or it can't.

Director: It's that simple?

Scientist: It's that simple. And that's what makes it beautiful.

Director: But what if you know, just know something is true — but can't prove it's so?

Scientist: I keep on trying.

Director: And if you keep on trying and trying, and there's still no proof?

Scientist: I don't understand what you're getting at.

Director: Isn't this the fate of certain visionaries? 'Knowing' but not quite having proof?

Scientist: Yes, but that's a precarious place to be.

Director: Why?

Scientist: Because science rightly disowns those who think they know but don't.

Mixed (Friend)

Friend: I think we can have mixed destinies.

Director: Mixed as in some good aspects and some bad?

Friend: Yes. What do you think?

Director: I think we certainly can. But I'd take it further.

Friend: How so?

Director: I'd say no one has, or ever had, or ever will have a perfectly good destiny.

Friend: I agree. But what about the opposite?

Director: A perfectly bad destiny?

Friend: Yes. Do you think it's possible to have one?

Director: I don't know. What would it mean to have a perfectly bad destiny?

Friend: It would mean that nothing ever would go right.

Director: Hmm. It seems likely that something, anything, would go right, if only once.

Friend: So everyone's destiny is mixed?

Director: Yes.

Friend: But there's mixed and then there's mixed. One part this to ten parts that. Or one part that to a thousand parts this. Do you know what I mean?

Director: Of course.

Friend: So for all practical purposes, if someone has one part good and ten thousand parts bad — can't we say this person's destiny is simply bad?

Director: We can, Friend. But it wouldn't strictly be true.

Friend: Then what do we have to do? Examine every part and spell things out?

Director: Yes. After all, we might discover something very interesting along the way. We might learn that one part good, truly good, can, for that person, outweigh a million parts bad. Or maybe it's more like one outweighs five. But you get the point. Yes?

Pure (Artist)

Artist: Mixed destinies are muddled. How can I be expected to write about them?

Director: You'd rather have a pure destiny to work with?

Artist: Any day.

Director: Even if you know there's no such thing as a pure destiny in real life?

Artist: Bah! Who cares? I'll exercise my artistic license and make the work clean.

Director: You know, many artists like to portray the mixed, the ambiguous.

Artist: Yes, and they think they're very clever, too. Give me unambiguous good or bad and I'll be happy.

Director: But what will you do with the facts that oppose you?

Artist: You mean the facts that scream out good or bad contrary to the bad or good I argue for? I'll explain them away as the exceptions that prove the rule.

Director: But what if there are a great many exceptions?

Artist: You mean the person's life was truly one great big mess? I just wouldn't write about someone like that.

Director: So on a scale of one to one hundred, bad to good destiny, you'd only write about those who fall between one and ten or ninety and one hundred?

Artist: Yes, something like that. I'd leave the teeming masses in the middle to someone else's devices. I want the extremes.

Director: But why?

Artist: Why? Ha! Because I don't want my message to be confused!

Director: You can only convey your message through cloaking the truth and making the extreme seem even more extreme?

Artist: Ah Director, I'll stop teasing you now. The best thing is to find what seems perfect, good or bad, and then to present the facts that challenge that view. In other words, you take down the 'simply good' and bring up the 'simply bad', if only a notch or two. That's what must be done. But I'll admit, such tedious work — is not at all to my taste!

RULES (SCIENTIST)

Scientist: It's some people's destiny to break the rules.

Director: Even in science?

Scientist: Yes, of course.

Director: But why would anyone want to break the rules in science?

Scientist: Because that's what it means to be creative.

Director: What happens when you break a rule?

Scientist: You might discover things that no one has ever seen or even thought of before.

Director: Just by breaking a rule?

Scientist: Don't get me wrong. The best rule breakers are those who know the rules best.

Director: You mean they know which rules to break?

Scientist: Precisely.

Director: But couldn't someone with no training as a scientist, with no knowledge of the rules, stumble into breaking a rule and discover something new?

Scientist: Yes, that happens.

Director: And is the end the same either way? Trained scientist or amateur stumbler?

Scientist: No, not quite.

Director: Why not?

Scientist: Because the trained scientist would have a better idea of how to make sense of things.

Director: What do you mean?

Scientist: Someone has to fit the discovery into science as a whole. In other words, someone has to make a new rule. So if it's your destiny to break and destroy, it might also be yours to step in and create our new perspective on things.

Grounded (Friend)

Friend: Facing the unknown is our greatest test.

Director: Why do you say that?

Friend: Because the unknown has the power to unnerve us.

Director: But can't the known also unnerve?

Friend: I suppose. But it's not the same. There's something about the unknown that makes it seem worse.

Director: Because of our imagination?

Friend: Yes. We always imagine the absolute worst. We obsess on the bad we foresee. And then we lose our confidence. And then we can't live our destiny.

Director: So what should we do?

Friend: Check our imagination.

Director: Hmm. I wonder. Does this mean those with no imagination are better off than those who have it?

Friend: Of course not. The more we can imagine the more we can do. Provided our imagination doesn't cripple us.

Director: How can we prevent that?

Friend: We can verify everything we imagine.

Director: And what about the times when that's not possible? When there are things we simply can't know?

Friend: We need to be grounded.

Director: What does that mean?

Friend: It means we need to know what we know and hold to it with all our might.

Director: And then let the unknown unfold?

Friend: Yes. And no matter what happens — we never let go.

Prudence (Artist)

Artist: Prudence generally isn't an exciting trait for artists.

Director: Why not?

Artist: Because prudence is boring.

Director: It's boring to live your life well?

Artist: Of course! Who wants to hear about that? People want to hear about the great gamblers. Win or lose, it doesn't matter. Just roll those dice!

Director: But what sort of life do these two opposite types of people have?

Artist: Typically? The prudent have a happy one — or at least one that's not so bad.

Director: But isn't there all the difference in the world between 'happy' and 'not so bad'?

Artist: No, there's all the difference in the world between 'miserable' and 'not so bad'.

Director: Whose lot is it to be miserable?

Artist: The one who bet it all and lost.

Director: But if that person bet it all and won? A happy fate?

Artist: No, to say 'happy' would be to lie.

Director: What then?

Artist: Elated.

Direction: Can elation last?

Artist: Not as long as misery can.

Director: Why then roll the dice? Why not be prudent?

Artist: Because not everyone can be that way.

Director: I don't understand.

Artist: It's simple, really. Destiny demands different things of us. Some must be colorful, and some must be drab.

GENEROSITY (SCIENTIST)

Scientist: No, I wouldn't say the generous always come to a good end.

Director: Why not?

Scientist: Because ingratitude seems to be the order of the day.

Director: Yes, I've often heard that. But tell me, Scientist. What's the opposite of generosity?

Scientist: Miserliness.

Director: Is there another opposite?

Scientist: I don't understand.

Director: What about extravagance? Giving too much.

Scientist: Giving too little on the one hand, and giving too much on the other — with perfect generosity in-between? I think that's a good way to look at this.

Director: And the generous, in the sense of the mean between the extremes — would you say they deserve to come to no bad end?

Scientist: Yes, I would. And I'd even say that if they give just the right amount, they deserve to come to a good end.

Director: Regardless of gratitude?

Scientist: Let's just say people of such generosity appreciate a healthy bit of gratitude — but don't depend on it in any fundamental way.

Director: What about people of extravagance?

Scientist: I think it's fair to say that such people depend too much on gratitude. And I think we can also say the miserly don't care about gratitude at all, when they should to some degree.

Director: Oh, but is that true? Don't the miserly care too much? Isn't fear of lack of proper gratitude the very reason they don't give?

Scientist: Not the misers I know, my friend. They don't give — because they'd rather have!

Love (Friend)

Friend: Love is destiny.

Director: But what does that mean?

Friend: Anyone who is in love and has that love returned walks with destiny.

Director: It's as simple as that?

Friend: It's as simple as that.

Director: Then we have nothing more to say.

Friend: Oh, but we can say more. We can say what destiny means.

Director: Does it mean we've found happiness? That happiness and destiny are one?

Friend: Of course not. For destiny to be one with happiness you need certain circumstances.

Director: I'm not sure I understand.

Friend: Destiny alone doesn't bring happiness. You can walk with it and still be miserable. Just imagine. You might have famine, disease, war, and so on, and so on.

Director: Oh. I would have thought that in speaking of the destiny born of love, the miserable circumstances might be less extreme, such as differences in character, beliefs, and taste.

Friend: A good point. Differences in those things are hard to overcome.

Director: Hard but not impossible?

Friend: Yes.

Director: And what about the other circumstances? Disease and so on? Hard but not impossible to overcome?

Friend: You can love and have your happiness marred by things beyond your control.

Director: Yes, that's true. So is there a lesson we can draw from all this?

Friend: We should be grateful for any happiness in love we have.

PRIDE (ARTIST)

Artist: When you walk with destiny, how should you carry yourself?

Director: If you want to be an interesting character?

Artist: Yes.

Director: Then with pride.

Artist: Why pride?

Director: Artist, don't you know?

Artist: Tell me.

Director: You'll be like a lightning rod. What's more interesting than that?

Artist: And if you carry yourself meekly?

Director: Then what kind of destiny do you think you can have?

Artist: Ha! That sounds like something I would ask.

Director: Then you should be able to answer it.

Artist: Alright. If you're meek, your destiny is to be tread upon.

Director: But if you're tread upon, are you really walking with destiny?

Artist: No, you're not. You're slithering with destiny.

Director: What animal slithers?

Artist: You know as well as I — the snake.

Director: Are snakes all meek?

Artist: Not when they bite.

Director: Do you think it's the destiny of some of the meek to bite?

Artist: Well, now that I think of it, it might well be!

Director: So what sort of fool treads on the meek?

Artist: The sort that doesn't know that the meek, too, like their revenge.

Humility (Scientist)

Scientist: Some of those with the greatest destinies in science are the most humble.

Director: They're aware of the vastness of the universe and how little we actually know?

Scientist: Yes, precisely.

Director: But does that make them humble or realistic?

Scientist: Well, yes — you have a point.

Director: So some of those with the greatest destinies in science are the most realistic?

Scientist: I think that's true.

Director: And to be sure, are realism and humility the same thing?

Scientist: No, they're not.

Director: Which would you rather be? Realistic or humble?

Scientist: I'd rather be both.

Director: But if you had to choose?

Scientist: I believe it's best to be realistic.

Director: Why?

Scientist: Because when you're realistic, you're always humble. But when you're humble, you're not necessarily realistic.

Director: But why?

Scientist: You might be too humble.

Director: And you can never be too realistic?

Scientist: No, never.

Director: So tell me. If you're unrealistic about yourself, what happens?

Scientist: You either think too well or too poorly of yourself. And in either case — you do harm.

ANIMALS (FRIEND)

Friend: Do animals have destinies, or is it just humans that do?

Director: I don't know, Friend. What do you think?

Friend: I think animals do. It's arrogant to think that only we humans have destinies.

Director: I wonder if many animals think we don't have destinies, the way that many humans think animals don't.

Friend: I think animals think humans have destinies just like they do.

Director: So the error is only on one side?

Friend: Yes.

Director: Do people who see the mistake have an obligation?

Friend: I think they do. They have a duty to respect animals.

Director: A duty to respect animals with good destinies? Or all animals?

Friend: How can humans tell what kind of destiny an animal has?

Director: The same way an animal can tell what kind of destiny a human has.

Friend: How?

Director: Each can tell when the other thrives or has the potential to thrive.

Friend: That's all you think it takes to have a good destiny?

Director: You don't think it's a good indicator?

Friend: It just seems... too simple.

Director: Aren't most animals simple in nature?

Friend: True. But not all humans are.

Director: Would you say that the more complicated people are, the harder it is for them to thrive?

Friend: You know, I would. So maybe we need to simplify ourselves, down to the essential in certain things — and emulate animals as far as this goes.

Abandoned (Artist)

Artist: Tell me about feeling abandoned by destiny.

Director: It's quite simple, really. You feel yourself walking with destiny for a good long while. And then one day you realize — it's gone.

Artist: But what changed? Why are you now alone?

Director: Who can say?

Artist: But you've lost your purpose, your drive?

Director: Yes, of course. You're lost without your destiny.

Artist: But that can't be true.

Director: Why not?

Artist: I never walked with destiny. And I'm not lost.

Director: Yes, but you don't have a void.

Artist: The void that destiny left when it went away?

Director: Yes. And there's no void more terrible than that.

Artist: Well, the abandoned need to fill that void.

Director: With what?

Artist: With art, for instance. Or whatever else they can find.

Director: I don't know. I think it's rare to fill the void.

Artist: So what do you suggest these people do?

Director: Find their destiny once more.

Artist: And do what? Hope it never abandons them again?

Director: Artist, you know the truth. Destiny never abandons you. You always abandon it.

Artist: If that's true, then when those who abandoned destiny take it up again, they should apologize to themselves at once — and get back to walking their way.

Humor (Scientist)

Scientist: It's important to have a sense of humor about your destiny.

Director: Why?

Scientist: Because there will be times when things don't go well.

Director: And you need to be able to take these things lightly?

Scientist: Precisely.

Director: Well, that makes good sense. But what if they're important things?

Scientist: If they already haven't gone well, will taking them too seriously make them any better?

Director: You have a point. So when should you take things seriously?

Scientist: In the planning and execution.

Director: And then whatever happens, happens?

Scientist: Yes.

Director: This seems good advice for scientists when it comes to experiments, even very expensive experiments. If things don't go well, it's disappointing. But there will be other experiments to conduct and new hopes for success. But do you think that's how it is with everything?

Scientist: Of course it's not. There are times when lives are at stake.

Director: In such a case, after you've planned and executed in all seriousness to the best of your ability, and lives are lost — I assume you mean humor is never appropriate.

Scientist: Without a doubt.

Director: Can you put your finger on why that is?

Scientist: Because it would show a lack of respect.

Director: What would show respect?

Scientist: To honor the dead. And then to make a solemn vow, a promise on oath — to do all you can so that this never, but never, happens again.

DETACHMENT (FRIEND)

Friend: A sense of detachment from your destiny? I'm not sure how that would be good.

Director: Why not?

Friend: Because it's like not paying attention to the road while you're driving. Isn't it?

Director: I don't know. Maybe it's like paying more attention to the road.

Friend: How so?

Director: If we're always completely focused on our destiny, what attention do we have left to focus on other things, like roads?

Friend: So you're saying that if we loosely focus on our destiny, we'll be better able to pay attention where needed?

Director: Yes. What do you think?

Friend: I think there's truth to that. We'll be attached to our destiny but not in an all consuming way.

Director: Good.

Friend: But aren't there times when we should allow our destiny to consume us?

Director: When would that be?

Friend: When we're alone and doing nothing else.

Director: That's probably safest, yes.

Friend: Yes. And that's when we can burn our destiny into our hearts and minds.

Director: Why do we need to do that?

Friend: So that it's always there, in the background of all we do!

Director: Meaning destiny sets the tone for everything that happens in the foreground of life?

Friend: Yes, exactly. In a way, it's the soundtrack to our lives.

Director: Hmm. But we should be careful the music doesn't carry us away.

Objectivity (Artist)

Artist: No, you can't be objective about your own destiny.

Director: Why not?

Artist: What's more personal and subjective than that?

Director: I'm not sure I understand. Are you saying others can be objective about your destiny?

Artist: No. Their understanding of your destiny is subjective, too.

Director: So no one can be objective about anyone's destiny?

Artist: That's right.

Director: Then it's a misguided effort to try to help someone see their destiny?

Artist: No, you can help them see — in their own way.

Director: And you'll see what they see in your own way?

Artist: You're quick learner, Director.

Director: I'm usually slow. It must be because of the ability of my teacher.

Artist: Ha! Well, yes — I can teach you about this.

Director: Then tell me, Artist. If our destiny is subjective, how can we know it's our destiny?

Artist: You want the validation of a witness. But you can't have it.

Director: Because, truly, all we have is our own subjective certainty?

Artist: Yes.

Director: But aren't lunatics subjectively certain about things in their own lives?

Artist: There's no essential difference between a lunatic and a person of destiny.

Director: How can that be?

Artist: Both have subjective certainty. It's just that one has better luck.

Sharing (Scientist)

Scientist: Director, do you think you can share your own destiny?

Director: Why do you ask?

Scientific: I'm thinking of getting married.

Director: Ah! Well, yes — I think you can have a shared destiny. I assume she has a career in science?

Scientist: Yes, she does — in my field. But I didn't ask about 'a shared destiny'.

Director: What do you mean?

Scientist: A shared destiny and sharing your own destiny are two different things.

Director: Are you suggesting that a marriage can have three destinies? The shared destiny and the two individual destinies?

Scientist: I am. And I'd rather there be only one.

Director: Well, what stops you from making this so?

Scientist: I'm not sure there's a way to subsume the individual destinies into the shared destiny.

Director: Have you talked about this with your love?

Scientist: I haven't.

Director: Why not? Are you afraid she'll want to keep her individual fate?

Scientist: I am, Director. And I don't know how to broach the topic with her.

Director: Tell me. Why do you want her to share her individual destiny with you?

Scientist: Because if I share mine, too, then we'd have everything in common.

Director: But that might not be what she wants?

Scientist: That's the terrible thought I have. Do you think I'm being foolish?

Director: I think you're being a touch controlling, my friend. But you need to talk to her. Because who knows? She might be that way, too.

Signs (Friend)

Friend: I think a lot of people want to keep silent about their destiny.

Director: Why?

Friend: They're afraid of it.

Director: Afraid of it? How so?

Friend: They're superstitious.

Director: One wrong word and you might curse yourself to a bad destiny?

Friend: Exactly.

Director: But maybe it's not so bad.

Friend: What do you mean?

Director: Maybe the wrong word is only a sign.

Friend: A sign of what? A destiny that's gone off course?

Director: Yes. And aren't we all on the lookout for signs like this?

Friend: But that's just it. People don't want their bad signs on display.

Director: But a bad sign can help you find your way.

Friend: But why do others need to know?

Director: They keep you honest, so to speak.

Friend: So we're saying better a bad sign than no sign at all?

Director: Of course. How else can we diagnose what's going on?

Friend: Because a bad sign is a symptom of a sort of illness?

Director: Yes, and illness as far as destiny goes is a very serious thing.

Friend: Then who's the doctor who can help?

Director: Someone who knows a thing or two about how signs and destinies relate.

Friend: Then that 'someone' would be you.

Confessions (Artist)

Artist: Would I ever write a tell-all book of confessions? Of course not. It's not my destiny to show just how boring my life has really been! Would you?

Director: You think my life is exciting?

Artist: Well, let's see. All you do is go around talking to people. I suppose some conversations are more exciting than others. But on the whole? Exciting?

Director: I think it is.

Artist: Ha! Your threshold for excitement must be much lower than mine.

Director: That may be. But I don't think I'd write the book.

Artist: Why not? Maybe there are other low threshold people out there who'd love to read it.

Director: But why write for them when I can talk to them?

Artist: Yes, but a book lives beyond what you alone can reach.

Director: Yes, and a book says everything to everyone.

Artist: What do you mean?

Director: If I confess something to someone, I have confidence that the person won't betray my trust. No?

Artist: Of course.

Director: But just because I trust someone with one thing doesn't mean I'd trust them with everything. True?

Artist: True. The ones you trust with everything — if they exist at all — are rare.

Director: Well, what happens when you send a book out into the world that everyone can read? Are you just trusting indiscriminately?

Artist: No. The trust is in your art. Good art says different things to different people, my friend. It speaks to all and none.

Director: Even in the confessional? Then teach me this good art, my friend. And then I'll consider how bold in the telling to be.

Fame (Scientist)

Scientist: To wish for a destiny of fame is the height of foolishness.

Director: Why?

Scientist: Because fame is an ordeal.

Director: So why do people wish for it?

Scientist: They must imagine it's other than it is.

Director: Yes, or maybe they're masochists. But what about you, Scientist?

Scientist: What about me?

Director: If fame comes would you accept it?

Scientist: What choice would I have?

Director: You could let your work speak for itself.

Scientist: You mean my work would be famous but not me?

Director: Yes.

Scientist: No, that's not how it works.

Director: Why not?

Scientist: My work... is me!

Director: So you'd better be careful not to do too great a job.

Scientist: Ha, ha.

Director: I'm serious. If you do an amazing job, and fame sweeps you up, where will you be?

Scientist: You have a point, of course. So what's the answer?

Director: Work on meaningful but somewhat obscure problems. And then you can win the admiration of some of your peers without broader fame.

Scientist: And that's what you do with your philosophy? Well, if I take that path I know I'll be in good company. And who knows? We can always hope for fame... after death!

Weakness (Friend)

Friend: Do you think weakness makes for a bad destiny?

Director: Not always.

Friend: How?

Director: Suppose your weakness inclines you to be mild mannered and pleasant. And you live your life that way. And you have friends who love you. A bad destiny?

Friend: No, but I think it's different than how you describe it. It takes strength, inner strength, to remain mild and pleasant through both thick and thin — and all lives experience the thick and the thin.

Director: So what kind of weakness have you got in mind?

Friend: Giving in to peer pressure.

Director: Ah, I see. I think giving in all the time makes for bad destiny.

Friend: All the time? Do you think there are times when giving in is good?

Director: Well, let's consider. What is peer pressure?

Friend: Something that makes you do things you really don't want to do.

Director: Can you think of anything you really don't want to do that's good for you to do?

Friend: Of course. I often feel that I really don't want to go out for a run.

Director: If peer pressure makes you run, when you otherwise wouldn't have, does that make peer pressure good?

Friend: I want to agree, but I don't want to agree.

Director: Why?

Friend: Because it's better if I motivate myself!

Director: Agreed. But if you're too weak? Is it better not to run or to give in and run?

Friend: I suppose it's better to give in. But I can't believe you're arguing this way!

Director: Arguing that the weak give in and on occasion that's good? That's life.

Strength (Artist)

Artist: You can be strong and have a bad destiny.

Director: How?

Artist: Oh, so many ways! But here's my favorite. You can over-reach.

Director: Why is that your favorite?

Artist: Because then we get to see a great big fall!

Director: What's another way for someone strong to have a bad destiny?

Artist: The opposite. To under-reach.

Director: Then the secret must be to reach for just the right thing.

Artist: Of course. To the furthest extent of your strength.

Director: And if you reach for just the right thing, is your destiny necessarily good?

Artist: Succeed or fail? I suppose it is. There's something noble in failing while trying your best to achieve something worthy of your strength.

Director: So, Artist, what are you trying to achieve?

Artist: You know what I'm trying to achieve.

Director: Great art? But isn't there a risk you'll miss the mark? And then would you be content with the noble destiny of worthy failure?

Artist: You know I don't believe in destiny.

Director: Yes, but I'm starting to think I know what you do believe in.

Artist: What's that?

Director. Success.

Artist: Ha! You're right! And know this. Just making works like mine amounts to great success. A victory. So I'm beyond caring if my works all 'fail'. And that's my strength.

Director: That may be. But it sometimes seems that you... protest too much.

Artist: Well, that may be. But how else can I ensure the protest will be heard?

HOMOGENEITY (SCIENTIST)

Scientist: Some think a good destiny is to be with those who are the same.

Director: What's good about such a destiny?

Scientist: Comfort, the comfort of the herd.

Director: And herds are homogeneous?

Scientist: Yes, of course.

Director: What's the risk of homogeneity?

Scientist: An inability to adapt to changed circumstances through lack of diversity.

Director: So what do you recommend?

Scientist: Don't live your life among only those who are like you. Dare to branch out.

Director: And the life you save might be your own? But does this hold when it comes to choosing a mate? I mean if you're tall and fat, should you choose a mate who's short and thin?

Scientist: Now you're being ridiculous.

Director: Am I? What if I say this? If you're of fiery temperament, you should choose a mate who's steady and calm. Or do you think the fiery should mate with the fiery?

Scientist: Well, I think it's hard to say. So much else is involved.

Director: But you do think it's best to mate diversely?

Scientist: Yes. Too much is at stake not to be diverse.

Director: So what's the most important thing as far as diversity goes? In other words, in what way do we most differ from other human beings?

Scientist: I'm not sure. What do you think?

Director: Isn't it in what we believe?

Scientist: I suppose that's true. But if mates don't share beliefs, then what's the glue to hold them together? And if nothing holds them together — then what's the point?

BECOMING (FRIEND)

Friend: It's good to be broad minded, to associate with those who are different than you.

Director: Blend the strengths, as they say? Enhance your destiny?

Friend: Yes. But too much difference for too long can be tiresome. You never get a rest from dealing with the other.

Director: You can only rest in the same, the ones like you?

Friend: I hate to say it, but yes. It's exhausting to deal with the different all the time.

Director: So work your way up.

Friend: What do you mean?

Director: Your tolerance. Start out small with those unlike yourself. Then take a break. Then increase how much time you spend with them. Then take a break. And so on.

Friend: But where does it end?

Director: You tell me.

Friend: Eventually I might spend more time with them than with the ones like me!

Director: And what then? Are you worried you might become unlike the ones like you?

Friend: Do you think I might?

Director: In some ways. But not essentially. It's very rare, if it ever happens at all, for someone's essence to change. But that's not to say you might not have a change of heart.

Friend: And then what happens?

Director: You become unlike the ones you once were like, concerning matters of the heart.

Friend: But what if I have another change of heart? And another? Then who am I like?

Director: If your heart is changing often, you might be posing the wrong question. Instead of asking who you're like, ask who you love. And then associate with them, regardless of how like they are to you or not. Eventually, your heart will find its peace.

OUR WAY (ARTIST)

Artist: Sure, some people think their destiny is through others, especially through their children.

Director: But what if their children think the exact same way?

Artist: And so on, and so on?

Director: Yes. Where's the destiny? It's always receding.

Artist: Yes, it's always delayed to some time in the future.

Director: But if it's not? If someone finally says, My destiny is with me?

Artist: Then destiny is at long last in the now.

Director: How hard would it be for people of such a lineage to live their destiny in the now?

Artist: I think it would be the hardest thing they could ever do. Think of all that momentum built up over generations pushing them to place their destiny somewhere else.

Director: As opposed to placing it in themselves.

Artist: Yes. But it's impossible to live through others. The attempt is doomed to fail.

Director: Destiny is ours, and ours alone?

Artist: Of course it is.

Director: And what if someone, anyone, tries to climb on in?

Artist: We have to push them out.

Director: And if we don't?

Artist: We commit the ultimate sin.

Director: The ultimate sin? What's that?

Artist: I'm sure you know full well.

Director: We fail to go our way.

SECRECY (SCIENTIST)

Scientist: Why would people hide their destiny?

Director: Maybe they believe it will be looked down upon, will be unpopular, and so on? And maybe they believe there will be those who actively oppose them.

Scientist: So their strategy is to hide — because they're weak?

Director: Weak, or simply overwhelmed.

Scientist: But then they'll never achieve their destiny! Destiny isn't destiny unless it shows itself in the full light of day.

Director: You don't have to persuade me. But why do you think that is?

Scientist: Because, simply, destiny doesn't belong to the night.

Director: Yes, Scientist, but why doesn't it belong to the night?

Scientist: Since you say you don't need persuading that destiny belongs to the light, you tell me.

Director: Hmm. Maybe we need an experiment to prove what we think. Let's take two things that claim to be destinies, one that's already in the sun and one that hides in a cave. We'll switch them up and see how they do.

Scientist: So if the one from the sun was thriving in the sun but wilts in the cave, that's evidence that sun is best?

Director: Yes. And if the one from the cave thrives in the sun? Again, we see evidence that sun is best.

Scientist: But what if the one from the cave was thriving in the cave?

Director: Well, then it seems we've found a destiny that is in fact destiny despite the fact it doesn't show itself in the full light of day.

Scientist: But how do we know it's destiny? What if it's actually something else?

Director: What else could it be? What looks like destiny but isn't?

Scientist: Imaginary destiny, 'destiny' that exists only in your head.

Director: And you think that can make you thrive? We'd better check that cave again.

Openness (Friend)

Friend: When can you be completely open about your destiny? I'm not sure you ever really can.

Director: Why not?

Friend: Well, for one, people will laugh at you. There's something ridiculous about declaring your destiny to all.

Director: It will seem like you're boasting, yes? And will it seem like foolishness?

Friend: Yes, like foolishness. Because you'll be giving your enemies an opportunity to oppose you.

Director: Because if they know what you think your destiny is, they know what you're likely to do, and can anticipate and interfere? But what about with your trusted friends? Can you be open with them?

Friend: Aside from someone like you? I don't know. I mean what if you think you have a destiny of greatness and your friends think their own destinies are less than that?

Director: Your friends will feel inferior? If that's true then I can see why you might not want to speak freely. But maybe there's a way.

Friend: How?

Destiny: Well, we need to be very sure we know our destiny first. And then we need to be aware of the risk that we won't live up to it. This awareness will temper us. And if we're properly tempered, is there anything we can't say?

Friend: But, Director, when you're tempered like that you're not fully open.

Director: Do you think by 'open' we mean gushing out everything we think?

Friend: I think that's what some people think openness means.

Director: And will you take your bearings from what 'some people' think?

Friend: No. I'll take them from what I myself think.

Director: Good. Then there's hope for you.

Friend: Good. But I didn't know that was in doubt.

Loud (Artist)

Artist: Sure, the louder the better. Trumpet your destiny! That gives people like me plenty to say.

Director: That's the thing, isn't it? Giving you plenty to say?

Artist: Of course! Look, you can't be afraid of what I or others will say. Some will say good things, others will say bad. What difference does it make?

Director: I suppose you need a thick skin.

Artist: Not if you just ignore what everyone says.

Director: I thought that's what it means to have a thick skin.

Artist: No, Director. Having a thick skin means to listen, and listen closely, and then not to get upset.

Director: If someone with a thick skin trumpets their destiny, do you listen closely?

Artist: Of course I do. And then I make fun.

Director: That doesn't sound very helpful.

Artist: Oh, but it is! If you're serious about your destiny, you have to learn what it means to be an object of fun.

Director: Why?

Artist: So you can gain perspective on yourself.

Director: After the fun, what else do you say?

Artist: I offer my serious view on their way.

Director: You mean whether it's bad or good?

Artist: Of course not! That's for them to decide. I talk about what it takes to succeed.

Director: And after that?

Artist: What else is there after that? Comedy and how-to advice. That's all you need. And you get it for free! Well, almost free. You just have to open your mouth and shout: This is my way! And then pay close attention to me.

Quiet (Scientist)

Scientist: I think it's best to be open about what you take to be your destiny but to speak quietly about it.

Director: Don't attract any undue attention? Why not?

Scientist: Because attention will bring distractions.

Director: Even if it's just others offering their advice?

Scientist: That can be most distracting of all.

Director: But can't you benefit from the counsel of others?

Scientist: Yes, but you don't want those others to be loud mouths.

Director: You mean, why let the word spread to unsympathetic ears?

Scientist: Precisely.

Director: But what if mixed among the unsympathetic there's a sympathetic ear or two?

Scientist: I'd still be wary. Destiny is a delicate thing. It involves what you think about yourself, your role, your place in the universe.

Director: And the sympathetic don't know all that?

Scientist: If they do, then why are they among the unsympathetic?

Director: Do you really think the world can divide itself neatly into those who sympathize with you and those who don't?

Scientist: No, you have a point. Only those with great hubris think that way.

Director: Then I think you should neither shout nor whisper your destiny. Just talk in a normal voice.

Scientist: And if the unsympathetic overhear and have something to say?

Director: Listen to them. And then politely repeat what you said.

Scientist: I don't know if I'd have the patience for that.

Director: Then that's the limit to what you can say.

Partnerships (Friend)

Friend: I think we can help each other achieve our destiny.

Director: How can we do that?

Friend: We form partnerships.

Director: And how long do these partnerships last?

Friend: They might be very brief or they might last a lifetime. It all depends.

Director: On whether both partners feel the partnership is beneficial?

Friend: Yes.

Director: What happens if one partner gets something out of it and the other doesn't?

Friend: Unfortunately, sometimes the partnership goes on.

Director: Why would it go on?

Friend: Because one party gets lost in the destiny of the other and forgets its own way.

Director: So they walk together but only one is walking with destiny?

Friend: Exactly.

Director: And do you think this happens all the time?

Friend: All the time.

Director: Well, that's a shame. What can we do?

Friend: Help to break the partnership up.

Director: You'd interfere like that?

Friend: Of course I would! Destiny is at stake.

Director: But how do you know which partner walks with destiny and which one doesn't?

Friend: Does it matter?

Director: Why wouldn't it matter?

Friend: Because when the partnership ends, both former partners should feel more free.

Marriages (Artist)

Artist: Yes, yes — our destiny is ours alone. But we can build destinies beyond ourselves. Think of my work. And think of marriages. The best are their own destiny. And in the best of the best the marriage has its destiny and each partner walks with an individual destiny, a destiny that's all their own.

Director: In that case it's double destiny for each? Both marriage and individual?

Artist: Yes.

Director: And if it's not?

Artist: The marriage will have some degree of trouble.

Director: When a marriage has trouble, what's usually the case? That it lacks the destiny of the marriage, or that it lacks each partner's individual destiny?

Artist: There are three ways of trouble. First is the failure of the marriage as its own destiny. Second is when neither partner has an individual destiny. Third is when one partner has an individual destiny and the other doesn't.

Director: Which way is worst?

Artist: They're all bad. But the worst is when one has a destiny but the other doesn't.

Director: And this could happen in a marriage that either has its own destiny or doesn't?

Artist: Yes. The point is the same either way, but easier to see in the case of the latter.

Director: Okay. But why do you say it's worst when one has destiny and the other doesn't?

Artist: Because the one that doesn't will impede the one that does.

Director: But in that case isn't it the same as when neither partner has a destiny?

Artist: No, it's worse. What's more terrible than having a destiny and having someone interfere, than having a destiny and having someone drag it down?

Director: I take your point. So tell me. What if there's no destiny to the marriage, and neither partner has an individual destiny? What have the partners got then?

Artist: They've got nothing. And, sad to say, such marriages often last.

Patience (Scientist)

Scientist: We won't always feel that we're walking with destiny.

Director: Even when we are?

Scientist: Yes.

Director: So what do we do when we feel that way?

Scientist: We have to be patient.

Director: And eventually the good feeling comes back?

Scientist: Don't you think it does?

Director: I'm not sure. How would we know? I mean what if a good feeling comes along and we think it's destiny but it's not?

Scientist: Maybe we don't know by feel.

Director: Then how do we know?

Scientist: Through reason.

Director: We can reason our way to destiny?

Scientist: I think we can.

Director: But does reasoning feel a certain way?

Scientist: I suppose it does.

Director: And if we reason well about destiny, we'll feel something good?

Scientist: Yes. And the feeling will truly be linked to destiny, not some mistake.

Director: So if we don't feel like we're walking with destiny, it might be because we're either not reasoning or not reasoning well?

Scientist: True.

Director: Then why do we need to be patient?

Scientist: Because reason takes time.

Manipulation (Friend)

Friend: I don't like to say it's ever right to manipulate someone.

Director: Not even if we have to do so in order to walk with destiny?

Friend: That's not the kind of destiny I'd want.

Director: But do you think it happens?

Friends: Happens that certain people's destiny requires them to manipulate others? I want to say no, but I'm afraid I have to say yes.

Director: What kind of people do you think might have to do this?

Friend: Politicians.

Director: Yes, that seems likely. But what about statesmen? Or don't you think there's a difference between the two?

Friend: There is a difference. Politicians manipulate but statesmen don't.

Director: That may be. But we'd better make sure we're clear. What does it mean to manipulate people?

Friend: To control and maneuver them.

Director: So that's what we're saying politicians do. But what do statesmen do?

Friend: They just maneuver without the control.

Director: And when they maneuver, maybe they do so with the consent of the maneuvered?

Friend: Yes, I like that.

Director: And what about this? Can we say that politicians don't regard the destiny of those they manipulate? They just use them however they will?

Friend: Of course we can say that.

Director: But statesmen, they pay careful attention to the destiny of those they maneuver, those they engage. They don't just use them however they will.

Friend: I agree completely. And so we've made clear the requirements for the job.

RECOGNITION (ARTIST)

Artist: True art is often doomed not to be recognized.

Director: You really don't believe that all good art must somehow, someday achieve recognition?

Artist: No, I don't. Some art is simply lost.

Director: The public never gets to appreciate it?

Artist: The public? Ha!

Director: Why do you laugh?

Artist: Because widespread recognition isn't always the artist's aim.

Director: If not that, then what is the aim?

Artist: Recognition by the few.

Director: The few who?

Artist: The few who know!

Director: Know a good thing when they see it? But what about the artists? How do they know when their work is good?

Artist: Don't you dare suggest that artists know it's good because the few say it is. No, you know your work is good when it can teach your intended audience how to appreciate your craft.

Director: How can it do that?

Artist: By gently persuading the audience to think different thoughts, thoughts they wouldn't have otherwise had, thoughts that build upon each other, and lead to the grand conclusion of the work — all of which, if they follow along, makes them see the merit of your work. That, my friend, is what it takes to be good.

Director: But tell me this. What if an artist does all you say with thoughts — but has no grand conclusion?

Artist: Many will never forgive you for that. But others? They appreciate a subtle touch at the end.

CREATIVITY (SCIENTIST)

Scientist: The creative don't always have good destinies.

Director: Why do you think that is?

Scientist: Sometimes the creative temper puts the person out of touch with the times.

Director: And we know what happens to those who do nothing but swim against the tide of the times?

Scientist: Precisely.

Director: So are you saying creative people will have good destinies if they swim with the tide?

Scientist: No, then there's nothing special about them.

Director: So they must swim against the tide at times. But how will they know when it's time?

Scientist: They'll know it's time when the temptation is greatest to swim with.

Director: Then does it follow that when the temptation is greatest to swim against, it's time to swim with?

Scientist: No, of course not.

Director: Why not?

Scientist: Because there's a reason they're tempted to swim against the tide.

Director: What reason?

Scientist: They want to give birth to the future.

Director: Swimming against the tide creates the future?

Scientist: Of course it does.

Director: What proof do you have?

Scientist: None — except for the whole history of the world.

Director: Well, that's an awfully strong tide to fight.

THE TIMES (FRIEND)

Friend: I think those with better destinies adjust with the times.

Director: Things tend to go better when you're flexible? But what if the times are bad? Should you adjust yourself to them?

Friend: You mean become bad yourself? No, of course you shouldn't. You just have to resign yourself to having a worse destiny than those who adjust.

Director: But, Friend, are you suggesting what I think you're suggesting?

Friend: What do you think I'm suggesting?

Director: That in bad times a good person can have a bad destiny and a bad person can have a good destiny.

Friend: Well, don't you think it's true?

Director: Hmm. Can you give an example of being good but having a bad destiny?

Friend: Sure. What if you're a martyr, suffering for the sake of what's good, and right, and true?

Director: Some people would say that's a good destiny.

Friend: Sure, the masochists. But what about the other way round? Being bad but having a good destiny. Do you think it's possible?

Director: I think there's a problem here. Bad people in bad times can suffer, too.

Friend: How do they suffer?

Director: By virtue of having sold themselves to the times. Deep down inside some of them can never forgive themselves for that. And so they take it out on others — especially those we might think of as saints.

Friend: Then what can we do if it's bad either way?

Director: Stand up for what's good — without sacrificing yourself.

Friend: But how can you do that? People will attack you for standing up.

Director: You just have to be resilient and find a way to fight back and win. And that, my friend, is how times change.

Sacrifices (Artist)

Artist: A good destiny is worth making sacrifices for. And sometimes we have to sacrifice one destiny to another. But how do we know it's time for that? There will be signs.

Director: What signs?

Artist: The new destiny will feel more important.

Director: What else?

Artist: It will be a better fit.

Director: As in more comfortable?

Artist: Yes, yes. But that's not to say it's without pains.

Director: More pains than the old destiny or fewer pains?

Artist: That's a difficult question.

Director: Why? If something fits, is comfortable, doesn't it involve fewer pains?

Artist: Yes, but you can be mostly comfortable but then at times feel greater pain.

Director: I see. Now, you don't claim to have a destiny. But as an artist you guide the ones who do. So how do you lead someone from an old destiny into the new?

Artist: Isn't it obvious from what we've said? You appeal to importance first, and then, in passing, to the better fit. It works like a charm. And who can say what drove the person to change? Was it longing for the importance of the new destiny? Or was it hopes of comfort? Did I perhaps suggest there'd no doubt be much less pain? If so, then that's my little lie. But noble spirits, they don't care about the pain. And so I tell them only truth.

Director: That's good practice.

Artist: Why do you say that?

Director: Because if you should ever choose to sacrifice your current way for destiny, then telling truth is where we'd start.

Artist: 'We'd' start? You mean you'd coach me toward my destiny? Ha! Well, a truthful start is fine. But then you'd better be prepared for many lies and obfuscations, friend. Because someone like me would need these things — to keep him on his way!

One's Own (Scientist)

Scientist: How do you find your destiny? Focus on the things that are properly your own.

Director: What's your own, Scientist?

Scientist: Mine? It should be obvious! Science. What's yours?

Director: Philosophy. Though I think I have more trouble with that than you do.

Scientist: What do you mean?

Director: Everyone agrees that what you do is science. No?

Scientist: Of course.

Director: Not everyone agrees that what I do is philosophy. In fact, many of those who call themselves philosophers would say that I don't 'do philosophy' at all.

Scientist: Why not?

Director: Because they see there's a difference between theirs and mine.

Scientist: What's 'theirs'?

Director: Something more than the dialogues in which I engage.

Scientist: But what more?

Director: I know it when I see it. Does that ever happen to you with science?

Scientist: No, never. I mean sure, there are scientists who aren't as rigorous as I am. And sometimes that makes me feel like we're working at cross purposes. But we're still kin, still engaged in the same basic enterprise.

Director: Well, that's just it. The other philosophers don't always engage in the same basic enterprise with me. And so I'd say they're not my kin.

Scientist: But maybe that can be your destiny! You'll be the one who finds the things that both you and they can share.

Director: I don't think they'll want to share unless I play their game.

Scientist: Then, Director — you must teach them it's no game.

PHILOSOPHY (FRIEND)

Friend: Is philosophy your destiny?

Director: Yes.

Friend: How do you know?

Director: Every time I try something different, philosophy calls me back.

Friend: So philosophy is your calling?

Director: Yes, that's fair to say.

Friend: But what exactly called you?

Director: Do you want me to say it was the voice of reason?

Friend: Is that what philosophy is? Listening to reason?

Director: In part.

Friend: What's the other part.

Director: Speaking reason.

Friend: Are those the only parts?

Director: No.

Friend: Then why don't you tell me what they are?

Director: I'm embarrassed to say it, Friend. But unless you already know what philosophy is, what I have to say about it won't make any sense.

Friend: Then tell me what philosophy is. And let me figure out the other parts myself.

Director: Philosophy is the attempt to know. That's as simple as I can say.

Friend: And you were making it sound so hard.

Director: You don't think it's hard to know?

Friend: Of course it is! But I'll tell you what's harder — getting others who don't want to know to know. And I suspect that's really what you think philosophy is.

Sphinxes (Artist)

Artist: Some artists like to pose riddles.

Director: Why do you think that is?

Artist: Mostly, it's because they think they're clever.

Director: What makes them think they're clever?

Artist: They pose riddles without answers and so, to many, they seem profound.

Director: But that's just a dirty trick.

Artist: Of course it is. And it means they have no destiny.

Director: Answers to their riddles would make them have destiny?

Artist: Yes. True riddles must have their answers. And if the riddles are very hard they make you a sphinx. What do you think is the destiny of a true sphinx?

Director: Its ultimate destiny?

Artists: No, the one before that.

Director: That's easy — to be ignored.

Artist: And what do you think its ultimate destiny is?

Director: Having someone guess the riddle?

Artist: No!

Director: But isn't that the point of posing a riddle? You want to get the answer back.

Artist: Yes, but you don't want someone to 'guess'. You want someone to know.

Director: So if I merely guess the riddle the sphinx won't acknowledge me?

Artist: Only if you prove that you know the answer, know it through and through, will a true sphinx recognize you.

Director: That makes it much harder for the sphinx to reach its ultimate destiny, no?

Artist: Of course. But it's that much better this way.

VAMPIRES (SCIENTIST)

Scientist: Energy vampires. I know they exist. They suck the life out of you just by being there.

Director: You mean they can't help themselves?

Scientist: No, I don't think they can. They're beyond all help. All they can do is prey upon others.

Director: So the big question is: Are you destined to be drained?

Scientist: Yes, that's it. And the other big question is: How to break yourself free?

Director: Just get up and leave.

Scientist: Ah, but it's never that easy.

Director: Why not?

Scientist: Energy vampires thrive on situations where things are complicated.

Director: You can still just get up and leave.

Scientist: Yes, I know what you mean. But when things are complicated it's like being caught up in a spider's web.

Director: Then cut yourself free.

Scientist: Yes, sure. Tell me, Director. Have you never been bitten by a vampire?

Director: The vampire bit, tasted my blood, and turned around and ran.

Scientist: Ha, ha! But really. Have you?

Director: That's a private matter, Scientist. I'd rather not say.

Scientist: Oh, I'm sorry. That's funny, though. I don't think I've ever heard you refuse to answer a question.

Director: What do you think it means?

Scientist: I think it means I've hit a nerve.

Director: Maybe. But at least that's better than hitting a vein.

Reminders (Friend)

Friend: I think we all need daily reminders in our lives about our destiny.

Director: Do you mean things we build into our day that will help keep us on track?

Friend: Exactly.

Director: But if we truly have a destiny, would we ever forget? Would we need reminders?

Friend: Maybe not. But what would it hurt to have them?

Director: It probably wouldn't hurt anything.

Friend: So how would you remind yourself about philosophy?

Director: I don't know. I've never thought about this before.

Friend: Maybe you could have philosophy books, prominently displayed on a bookcase in a room you're often in.

Director: That's not a bad idea.

Friend: Yes. And maybe you could write out quotations from your favorite philosophers and carry some of them in your pocket or your wallet.

Director: And change them up every so often to keep things fresh?

Friend: Exactly.

Director: And I could even give them out to friends, like the fortunes in fortune cookies!

Friend: Ha! I think you're getting the hang of this.

Director: Yes, and maybe that would inspire them to hand out philosophy fortunes, too! Would you?

Friend: Of course I would! I have a few philosophy books at home. I could copy out some sayings from the wise and carry them with me.

Director: But which would be your reminders? The ones you give or the ones you get?

Friend: The ones I get — from you! So choose them well, my friend. Choose them well.

Interests (Artist)

Artist: Follow them.

Director: Excuse me?

Artist: Your interests. Follow them.

Director: But first you have to know what your interests are.

Artist: Oh, we all know what our interests are, deep down inside.

Director: But we don't all follow them?

Artist: No, we don't.

Director: Why?

Artist: Because our interests generally speak in quiet voices. We hear them in our quiet times. And not all of us have quiet times — even when we're alone.

Director: So what are you saying, Artist? We know our interests but don't listen to them?

Artist: Yes, Director.

Director: So what do you recommend? Retreat from the noisy world?

Artist: No, not complete retreat. Only partial, like half an hour a day to meditate.

Director: Why not complete retreat? Would that mean you're weak?

Artist: No, just the opposite! Those who could stand a full retreat would learn to hear the quiet voice of interest, of destiny, all the time.

Director: And it takes strength to listen?

Artist: To listen all the time? Of course! Without that strength you'd end up going mad.

Director: And what about those in the world who never retreat in order to hear? Can't they go mad in their own way by virtue of not listening?

Artist: Yes, yes. But they have numbers on their side. So it's not as obvious with them.

Director: You mean they're mad but no one calls it what it is?

Artist: Yes, and that's the other thing they know deep down inside.

FEAR (SCIENTIST)

Scientist: Our fears lead us to our destiny.

Director: How do they do that?

Scientist: They drive us and they drive us, until we turn and face them.

Director: And when we've faced them?

Scientist: We see where we're supposed to be.

Director: And I take it that getting there isn't easy.

Scientist: It's the hardest thing in the world.

Director: Then it seems you've done the hardest thing in the world, my friend.

Scientist: Because I've achieved science as my destiny?

Director: Yes. But I'd like to know about your fears. What were you afraid of that led you here?

Scientist: Ah, Director — I'd rather not say. But what about you and philosophy? What fear was it that drove you there?

Director: Oh, but it wasn't fear.

Scientist: What was it, then?

Director: It was love.

Scientist: Love? But that can't be all.

Director: Why not?

Scientist: Because it must have been fear that drove you to love!

Director: Well, at least you're not saying it was love that drove me to fear.

Scientist: Ha, ha! Yes, that's true. But seriously, my friend. Look more closely into love and you will find you were led there by fear.

Director: Yes, Scientist, that certainly is a way of looking at the world. But I prefer to view things another way. And I often like what I see.

Hope (Friend)

Friend: Does walking with destiny always leave us hopeful?

Director: I think it depends on the destiny.

Friend: There can be a destiny without hope?

Director: I'm afraid so.

Friend: But then why have a destiny?

Director: Hope is that important?

Friend: Of course it is! Without hope you might as well be... dead!

Director: Hmm. What about those who do have hope? Is it possible for them to seem dead?

Friend: Well....

Director: Well?

Friend: Honestly? I've seen people with hope who seem dead.

Director: What makes them so?

Friend: They have hope, but the hope is without cause.

Director: You mean it's hopeless hope?

Friend: Exactly.

Director: So what are we saying? That there must be hope for our hope or else we're as good as dead?

Friend: Yes. And if only we could find a way to give the hopeless a hope that's true — we might be able to bring them back to life!

Director: How do we know when a hope is true?

Friend: There's a chance it might become real.

Director: Only a chance? Not a good chance?

Friend: Sometimes 'only a chance' is the best chance there is.

Individuals (Artist)

Artist: Only individuals can have a destiny.

Director: Can a corporation?

Artist: A corporation is an individual. Don't you know modern law? Artificial persons, these corporate beasts are called.

Director: Yes, and they can be immortal, too.

Artist: Are you suggesting they're our gods?

Director: No, but now that you mention it....

Artist: Let's get back to the point and focus on humans. Only individual humans can have a proper destiny.

Director: But that destiny can be fortified by a corporation, no?

Artist: Why are you stuck on this? Give me an example of how that would be.

Director: The examples are everywhere — and not limited to what we might strictly consider corporations. Consider a university. It fortifies the destinies of its professors.

Artists: Yes, yes. But they'd be better off teaching outside of the school.

Director: But then they'd lose their steady supply of students.

Artist: They'd just have to find them on their own. And if they find their own, they can be more selective. A university limits who you can teach.

Director: Don't all institutions limit who you can teach?

Artist: Of course. But all of this just confirms my prejudice.

Director: What prejudice is that?

Artist: That corporate persons, of whatever ilk, just get in the way of true individuals.

Director: Unless the true individuals run the corporations?

Artist: But even so, the true ones will eventually be swallowed up by the whale.

Director: Not if the whale doesn't like how they taste.

Applause (Scientist)

Scientist: Applause almost always distracts and misleads.

Director: How does it distract?

Scientist: Instead of focusing on your destiny, you focus on winning more applause.

Director: But what if it's your destiny to be applauded?

Scientist: There's always more to destiny than that — to a good destiny, anyway.

Director: Okay. But how does applause mislead?

Scientist: In the same basic way it distracts. Instead of following what you should follow, you follow any path that leads to praise.

Director: But what should you follow? Just any path that doesn't lead to praise?

Scientist: Of course not.

Director: What then?

Scientist: We need to clarify. What you should 'follow' is not to follow at all.

Director: I'm not sure I understand.

Scientist: You should blaze a trail.

Director: But won't you receive applause for doing just that?

Scientist: Sometimes, yes. Mostly, no. The true trail blazers often go out in anonymity.

Director: And the trail markings fade after they're gone?

Scientist: If they and their markings remain undiscovered for a long enough time? Yes.

Director: So why does one trail blazer win applause and another doesn't?

Scientist: Luck.

Director: Oh, I don't believe that's all you think. What does it take to win applause?

Scientist: Well, it's this. When you reach the end of your trail, you build a monument large enough to be seen a long way off. Many will be impressed. And then what do you think they'll do? They'll clap.

FALSE STARTS (FRIEND)

Friend: Do you think there's a limit to how many false starts we can have on the path to destiny?

Director: No, I don't think there's a limit. But if you use up all your time on false starts, you'll never really get anywhere.

Friend: True. But do you think sometimes it's our destiny to never really get started?

Director: Our destiny not to live our destiny? That doesn't sound right.

Friend: But what if we avoid what would otherwise have been a bad destiny this way? Wouldn't that somehow be good?

Director: You assume we'd know enough to see a bad destiny and avoid it?

Friend: I think we can sense when bad things await.

Director: If that's true, then why make false starts?

Friend: Because everyone likes to think great things will happen to them. And so they set out in confidence. But then they see bad things ahead and they stop and retreat. But then they remember great things should happen to them. And so they set out.

Director: Over and over? Hmm. I wonder. Couldn't a bad thing be like a bad dream?

Friend: You mean it's not real? I suppose it could be that way.

Director: How can we tell a dream from what's real?

Friend: I guess we'd have to go far enough down the path of destiny to know.

Director: But not so far that bad things happen to us if it turns out it's real?

Friend: Yes.

Director: Then is that what we'll advise? Go as far as you can without trouble?

Friend: Right. Dispel the bad dreams. But if what seems bad proves to be real...

Director: ...we run away? But why not fall back and prepare for battle instead? I mean, it's our destiny. Don't we have to do whatever we have to do in order to lay claim?

Friend: Yes, I know what you mean. But it's just that some of us aren't up for the fight.

PERSISTENCE (ARTIST)

Artist: I often feel like giving up on what I'm working on.

Director: What keeps you going?

Artist: Knowledge of what else is out there.

Director: And what else is out there?

Artist: Not much good.

Director: And by comparison your art doesn't seem so bad?

Artist: Right.

Director: Can you live with 'not so bad' as your work's destiny?

Artist: If everything else is 'not so good' and 'not so bad' is a step up in rank? Yes.

Director: Ah. Concerned with rank, are we?

Artist: What's wrong with wanting my work to be the best?

Director: Why can't you say 'among the best'?

Artist: Fine, fine. Among the best.

Director: After all, you don't want to be all alone. Do you?

Artist: I want to be alone enough that I can persist in my work.

Director: So how does it go? Persist, give up, look to others, become inspired, persist?

Artist: I didn't say I actually give up. I just feel like giving up.

Director: And is the work you create good when you're in this frame of mind?

Artist: I generally don't create when I'm in this frame of mind.

Director: So you stop?

Artist: 'Stop' implies I give up. I don't. And I won't. It's just sometimes I need a break.

Director: It's good you know when you need one, Artist. After all, who can work without end?

FLATTERY (SCIENTIST)

Scientist: Flattery doesn't always mislead? How can you say that?

Director: Well, it depends.

Scientist: On what?

Director: On whether you believe someone can be an expert — in your destiny.

Scientist: You mean someone might know your destiny as well as or better than you?

Director: Yes. Do you think it's possible?

Scientist: Let's say it is.

Director: And if someone knows your destiny, he or she could lead you to your destiny?

Scientist: Again, let's say the answer is yes.

Director: Now, suppose this person flatters you toward that end.

Scientist: But that's just the problem. What do you think flattery is?

Director: Making someone feel honored and pleased.

Scientist: That's not what flattery is.

Director: What is it?

Scientist: Praising someone insincerely.

Director: Do you think insincere praise can be effective praise?

Scientist: You mean in leading someone toward their destiny? No, of course not.

Director: So it's best for that purpose for praise to be sincere?

Scientist: Without a doubt. But, Director, why do you assume we have to praise in order to lead?

Director: Because praise is sweet and suggests that destiny too will be sweet.

Scientist: But what if the destiny proves not to be sweet at all?

Director: Then the memory of that sweet praise will turn bitter, my friend.

CONSCIENCE (FRIEND)

Friend: Is following your conscience enough to live up to your destiny?

Director: I think it can be.

Friend: Can be? Under what circumstances?

Director: If your conscience pushes you forward to act for good in addition to pulling you back to do no wrong.

Friend: But how does our conscience know when to push us forward?

Director: Well, maybe we have to train it.

Friend: I'm not so sure we can.

Director: Why? Do you think conscience is just an innate voice never to be changed?

Friend: Isn't it?

Director: Look at it this way. Can we reason with our conscience?

Friend: People who do that generally want to do something bad.

Director: But what if we don't want to do something bad?

Friend: We want to do something good? Then why do we need to reason with our conscience? It wouldn't object.

Director: But what if it does? There might be something wrong with our conscience. Or don't you think that's possible? Are all consciences made perfect from birth?

Friend: No, I don't think all consciences are perfect from birth.

Director: Well, what if your conscience thinks something good is bad?

Friend: I suppose you'd have to train it to see the good as good.

Director: Yes. And then you have to train it to speak in favor of the good.

Friend: But why must it speak? Silence implies consent.

Director: That's often true. But for some of us consent just isn't enough. We need encouragement. And why can't conscience serve us here?

Excuses (Artist)

Artist: People always make excuses not to follow their destiny.

Director: What's the biggest excuse?

Artist: That they don't know what their destiny is.

Director: But don't some people really not know?

Artist: Of course! But that's no excuse.

Director: It's everyone's duty to learn their destiny?

Artist: What greater duty does anyone have?

Director: You're saying this seriously?

Artist: I am — for almost anyone. Tell me. What greater duty do you have?

Director: None but to know and to live my destiny.

Artist: And you know your destiny?

Director: I do.

Artist: Then tell me what it is.

Director: Aside from philosophy in general terms? I'd rather not.

Artist: Superstitious, are you?

Director: No. It's just that if I tell you I'll have an excuse not to follow it.

Artist: I don't understand.

Director: If you knew my destiny, what might happen if you couldn't understand how a certain action of mine fit that destiny?

Artist: I might press you to explain.

Director: Right. And this may sound crazy, but the pain of having to explain might be enough to stop me from doing what I need to do. It would be my excuse.

Artist: I think I see the truth in that. After all, I would never want to have to explain my art each step along the way. So there — you're excused from opening up.

A Wider View (Scientist)

Scientist: The problem is that if we think of our destiny in very general terms we might not actually do anything to realize it.

Director: You mean it would be just a vague dream? But what if we have the opposite problem?

Scientist: We think of it in too much detail? I'm not sure that's possible. Detail is the key to destiny.

Director: But if we're very particular, wouldn't you say it's possible we might develop a somewhat narrow point of view?

Scientist: Yes, but that can be good, as in being focused.

Director: But, Scientist, what if something comes along, something that doesn't fit our rather narrow point of view — and it would help us toward our destiny? Might we overlook it?

Scientist: We might.

Director: So it's possible to have too narrow a point of view?

Scientist: I suppose that's true.

Director: Then how do we know when it's time to broaden our view?

Scientist: We know when we're feeling constrained.

Director: Our destiny should never constrain us?

Scientist: Let's say the fit should be snug. But it should feel comfortable and good. If not, then I'm with you. It's time to take a wider look around.

Director: And if when we take that look we come to see we're off the mark to some degree as concerns our way?

Scientist: And we're sure? Then we adjust.

Director: How?

Scientist: We find something particular, some important detail in our wider view that just seems right — and we focus there while we correct our course.

COURAGE (FRIEND)

Friend: You must be brave to follow your destiny — even if it's a bad destiny. There's a sort of honor in that.

Director: But, Friend, how can you say there's honor in following a bad destiny?

Friend: If it's your destiny, it's your destiny, Director. You have no choice in the matter. So you may as well follow it with honor.

Director: Well, you seem to have a point. Some of us do have bad destinies. But let's pass that over in silence for now. What kind of courage does it take to follow a good destiny?

Friend: What kind of courage? Isn't there only one kind?

Director: Why, no — or so it seems to me now.

Friend: What are the types of courage?

Director: There's courage concerning self, and there's courage concerning others.

Friend: How do they differ?

Director: With the one there are no witnesses, while with the other there are.

Friend: But I don't believe that's true.

Director: Why not?

Friend: If you're brave concerning yourself, while it's true no one might see that activity at the time, they will however see the end result.

Director: And what's the end result?

Friend: Confident steps toward your destiny.

Director: Tell me. What do you think it means to be brave concerning yourself?

Friend: To own up to who you are. Your strengths. Your limitations. Your weaknesses.

Director: It sounds like you think courage toward self is knowledge of self.

Friend: But it is! And ignorance of self is cowardice. And cowardice is just the thing that makes good destinies bad, and bad destinies worse.

COWARDICE (ARTIST)

Artist: True cowardice is hard to portray.

Director: Why is that?

Artist: Because cowards are expected to despise themselves.

Director: And they really don't?

Artist: Yes.

Director: But are you saying that they're proud?

Artist: No, no — of course not.

Director: I'd like to get a better sense of what you mean. So tell me. Are you a coward?

Artist: Well, that's rather a personal matter, don't you think? Are you?

Director: No.

Artist: And now I suppose I should ask if you're a liar, too! Ha! But seriously, who can tell with these things? Who can say with certainty, I am brave?

Director: You have a point. But tell me. Why don't cowards despise themselves?

Artist: Because they love themselves.

Director: But if they commit cowardly deed after cowardly deed — what's left to love?

Artist: Yes, that's a problem. But courage isn't the only thing to love about yourself. Can't you be cowardly and kind? If so, the cowards who are kind love the kindness in their souls. What do you think?

Director: I think you have a point.

Artist: Good! And there are other points. A coward can be just, a coward can be wise.

Director: But there are many who believe these things take courage, friend.

Artist: Sure, sure — everything takes courage. Even kindness, no? But courage alone can't make you just. And courage alone can't make you wise. We need something more. We need to know. We need to know what justice and wisdom call for in each particular case. And cowards can certainly know. What's in doubt is whether they'll act.

Purpose (Scientist)

Scientist: If you walk with destiny you're never bored.

Director: Not even if your destiny requires you to do boring things?

Scientist: Name something like that.

Director: Suppose you're a violinist and you must practice for hours each day.

Scientist: But the practice wouldn't be boring. You love to play!

Director: Well, suppose you're a teacher and you're teaching the same book to your students that you've taught for the last ten years.

Scientist: No, but you love the book! You love your students! That's not boring.

Director: How about this? You're a scientist and you must meticulously collect data from your experiment each day, every day, for years on end, with little or no change to what you see. Boring?

Scientist: But the purpose of the experiment is exciting!

Director: The purpose animates the doing?

Scientist: Yes, I think that puts it well.

Director: So are we saying that with a strong enough purpose, anything can be exciting?

Scientist: Don't you think it's true?

Director: I'm inclined to agree. So the hard part is finding purpose?

Scientist: Ah, but that's not so hard.

Director: Then why doesn't everyone have it?

Scientist: But they do!

Director: No one is ever bored?

Scientist: Of course not. People are bored. But it's because of cowardice. You see, we all have purpose deep inside. But few of us are brave enough to bring it out. And even when it's out, how many have the courage it takes to walk with it by their side?

Offense (Friend)

Friend: If you live in fear of offending others, you'll never reach your destiny.

Director: But if you live with no fear whatsoever of offending others, you'll also never reach your destiny. No?

Friend: Tell me why not.

Director: If you've offended everyone, who can you work with toward your destiny then?

Friend: I suppose you have a point.

Director: Maybe we can correct things by saying: Offend some if you must, but not others.

Friend: Yes, I think that's good.

Director: Then don't we need to know one thing?

Friend: What one thing?

Director: Whom we should offend.

Friend: No, I don't think it works like that.

Director: How does it work?

Friend: We go about our business, not intending to offend anyone, and some people are, inexplicably, offended.

Director: It's as simple as that?

Friend: Yes.

Director: But wouldn't it be better if we understood why some people are offended?

Friend: No, I don't think so.

Director: Why not?

Friend: Because then when we give offense, we do so knowingly!

Director: It's better not to know why we offend?

Friend: Yes. Because then we remain... innocent.

The Brash (Artist)

Artist: The brash can make for interesting characters.

Director: Oh, I thought they were rather predictable.

Artist: Yes, but put their predictability in just the right situation and — bang! Explosive.

Director: Is that their destiny then, to be placed in just the right situation?

Artist: Yes, and it takes an artist. But, I have to admit, they sometimes luck their way into placing themselves just so.

Director: Why would anyone want to become explosive?

Artist: Destiny is a war, Director. Sometimes you need a little kaboom.

Director: But who would you explode?

Artist: Who else? The idlers who stand in the way.

Director: I take it the idlers aren't living out their destiny?

Artist: Of course they're not! They need a wake-up call, and that's exactly what the brash can give.

Director: But do you think that's the only way to wake them up?

Artist: Don't you? Or would you try reasoning with them?

Director: I would try. But I'm aware some people need more than that.

Artist: Right. They need 'a reason'. And that the brash can give!

Director: But won't these people come to hate the brash?

Artist: Some will, yes. But you can't be brash and not expect to earn a little hatred along the way.

Director: So the brash are great agitators serving destiny's end?

Artist: Yes, they stir things up and set people going on their way.

Director: But do these stirred up people really know their way?

Artist: Maybe not at first. But give them time and see.

Tightrope (Scientist)

Scientist: Sometimes destiny requires that we walk a tightrope. The only way is straight ahead.

Director: Or backward.

Scientist: Well, yes — of course. But why would you set out on a tightrope and then decide to go back?

Director: Maybe you thought walking it would be easier than it was.

Scientist: Is that a good reason to go back? Because it's easier?

Director: Well, now that you mention it — I can't think of anything much harder than walking backward on a rope.

Scientist: Then why go back?

Director: Maybe you got close enough to the other side to see it's not for you.

Scientist: So you'd risk your life going back because it's not for you?

Director: Yes.

Scientist: What? Is it that simple to you?

Director: Simple to say, yes. Hard to do. But there's another way. We could somehow turn around on the tightrope before we start back.

Scientist: So instead of the constant danger of walking backwards on the rope, we'd have one great moment of danger, the moment when we turn, and then that's it?

Director: Are you forgetting that in walking a tightrope, even straight ahead, we risk our lives?

Scientist: No, I'm not forgetting that. But there are risks and then there are risks.

Director: So if we want to avoid the risk of turning around, we should be very sure we want to walk straight on ahead along the rope before we set out?

Scientist: Yes. And I think we should only set out when we already know what's on the other side.

Director: Ah, but Scientist — that takes away half the fun.

Specialties (Friend)

Friend: Sometimes it takes wide ranging interests to find your destiny. I mean you might not know what you're meant for unless you really look around.

Director: A good point. But what if it's your destiny simply to have wide ranging interests?

Friend: But then what can you say your destiny is?

Director: Why, to have a Renaissance mind. Don't you think that's a good destiny, Friend?

Friend: I suppose I do.

Director: So why not have that?

Friend: Because it's better to have something in particular.

Director: Why?

Friend: Aren't we always better when we specialize?

Director: Not necessarily.

Friend: Then why do so many talented people do so?

Director: I'm not sure they do.

Friend: What do you mean?

Director: The specialty we see might be only the tip of the iceberg of their interests.

Friend: True. But icebergs always have a tip.

Director: So we should always have something that others can see as our specialty?

Friend: Yes.

Director: Well, maybe as with the tip of an iceberg that just happens on its own.

Friend: You really think it might?

Director: Sure. So keep on searching out and building up your interests, Friend — and see if something special doesn't emerge.

YOUTH (ARTIST)

Artist: I think it's possible for someone to know their destiny from a very young age. And I think it's harder on them than on those who come to their destiny when mature.

Director: Why?

Artist: The mature are set in their ways. The young aren't.

Director: But don't we sometimes have to modify our ways to fit our destiny once we know it?

Artist: Yes, of course.

Director: And wouldn't that be generally easier for youths?

Artist: No, not at all.

Director: I don't understand.

Artist: When you've yet to set your ways you're all over the place.

Director: And being all over the place is hard?

Artist: No doubt.

Director: So the youths who know their destiny must struggle to get themselves under control so they can live the destiny they know they have?

Artist: You know that's not easy, don't you?

Director: Yes, I suppose do. But how is it with the mature? You know people will say it's harder on them because it's very difficult to change set ways.

Artist: Yes, yes. But when you're set in your ways you can work to modify one way at a time. You can proceed methodically. But if there's one thing most youths lack it's method. Everything is more chaotic with them.

Director: And the only way out of the chaos is to walk the path of destiny?

Artist: Yes.

Director: But once they're on their way surely the advantage goes to youth.

Artist: Of course. But youth is exceptionally good at squandering that.

Maturity (Scientist)

Scientist: Maturity means accepting the consequences of what you must do to follow your destiny.

Director: But do we have any choice but to accept them?

Scientist: Of course we do. We can fight against them. Haven't you seen people struggle this way, following their destiny but resisting what goes with it?

Director: Honestly? No, I haven't.

Scientist: Really? Then tell me why you think that is.

Director: Because the consequences are simply part of the destiny. If you fight them, you fight it. So those who struggle in this way aren't really following their way.

Scientist: You make it sound so simple.

Director: It's a simple thing. If you're following your destiny, you know that the consequences, even if some of them are unpleasant, are worth it.

Scientist: So what does that mean about maturity?

Director: It seems to mean that all of those who truly follow their destiny are mature. And do you know what else?

Scientist: No, what?

Director: It's true even when it comes to youths.

Scientist: The youths who follow their destiny are mature, are wise beyond their years?

Director: Well, that's an interesting question.

Scientist: Why?

Director: Because it suggests destiny and wisdom are one.

Scientist: But it also suggests maturity and wisdom are one.

Director: True. So it's very simple, no?

Scientist: Yes. What could be simpler than to say maturity and destiny and wisdom are one?

ENCOURAGEMENT (FRIEND)

Friend: I think sometimes we need to be encouraged by others to follow our destiny.

Director: But do you think it would be better if we could encourage ourselves?

Friend: Yes, of course.

Director: Why? Isn't encouragement encouragement?

Friend: Well, yes. But it's painful to have to be encouraged by another.

Director: Painful?

Friend: It's embarrassing.

Director: But don't you think we all need a hand from time to time?

Friend: Yes, but don't you know the reason why you'd need a hand when it comes to your own destiny?

Director: Tell me.

Friend: Laziness.

Director: We're too lazy to follow our own destiny and therefore need help to snap out of it and get moving on our way?

Friend: Exactly.

Director: But wouldn't walking our way more than make up for any embarrassment we may have felt for having been encouraged? Wouldn't we be proud to go our way?

Friend: You have a point.

Director: And isn't that so even when it wasn't simply laziness that was the cause of our falling short?

Friend: What other cause do you have in mind?

Director: Fear. You do think you can be afraid of your way, don't you?

Friend: I do. But it takes tremendous encouragement to help someone overcome fear.

Director: That may be. But once it's overcome isn't there even greater reason for pride?

GRATITUDE (ARTIST)

Artist: I'd go so far as to say that the only people we feel real gratitude toward are those who in some way helped us along our way — toward our destiny, I mean.

Director: Everything else isn't gratitude, it's just being polite?

Artist: Yes, you put that well.

Director: Thank you, Artist. But why do you think someone would want to help another in that way?

Artist: Now you're going to see just how simple minded I am.

Director: Why do you say that?

Artist: Because I believe, along with many others, that the more people who are walking their path to destiny, the better off is the whole world.

Director: That's an interesting belief for someone who claims to have no destiny.

Artist: Do you share it?

Director: I don't know. I'd have to think it through.

Artist: What's to think through? Do you want people floundering about, lost?

Director: Tell me, Artist. Do you believe there are people who are destined to do bad things?

Artist: Of course I do.

Director: And you think it's better for them to follow that destiny?

Artist: Yes. Because they bring things to a head. Then there's a sort of thunderstorm and then the air is cleared. Don't you want clear air?

Director: Yes, but I'm not sure that's the only way to get it.

Artist: How else? Would you persuade them not to follow their destiny?

Director: I'm not sure I could even if I wanted to.

Artist: And so the air will clear! But don't worry. You owe the bad no debt of gratitude. Clear air is nice, very nice — but who would say it helps you on your way?

SELFISHNESS (SCIENTIST)

Scientist: Is it selfish to pursue your destiny? Yes, profoundly. But what's the other choice?

Director: I'm not sure there is another choice, another good choice.

Scientist: Yes. And if we're all selfish, if we all pursue our own true destiny, doesn't that make for altruism?

Director: I'm not sure how that follows.

Scientist: Think of it this way. We're all running in a race. And we're all assigned a certain lane to run in. We run as hard as we can once the starter's gun goes off. That's the selfish part, running as hard as we can. But then we stay in our own lane, leaving others free to run in theirs. That's the altruism. What do you think?

Director: Altruism is following the rules?

Scientist: Yes.

Director: I don't know, Scientist. That doesn't seem very altruistic to me. ·

Scientist: What would seem altruistic to you, then?

Director: Turning around to go back and encourage the slower runners on.

Scientist: But you know that wouldn't really help them.

Director: Maybe it would make them feel better?

Scientist: Feel better that someone fast turned around and came back to help their poor selves out? Is it really helping them out? They won't run any faster.

Director: But maybe they won't give up.

Scientist: But maybe they should give up.

Director: And do what?

Scientist: Find another race, one they have a chance to win.

Director: So altruism is the weeding out of the weak?

Scientist: Well, when you put it like that.... I think our metaphor is somehow wrong.

FELLOW TRAVELERS (FRIEND)

Friend: Parting from fellow travelers when the time comes is hard.

Director: But it's harder to walk other people's path?

Friend: Yes, and no.

Director: And no? How so?

Friend: It's harder to walk other people's path because it never feels quite right. But it's easier to walk that path because you're just following along, making no real effort on your part.

Director: So how do you know when your path must branch off from those you're with?

Friend: If you're not paying attention you might not know at all.

Director: So what must you pay attention to?

Friend: Everything.

Director: But, Friend, how can you pay attention to everything?

Friend: You simply look about you with your eyes open wide.

Director: And that includes looking at your fellow travelers?

Friend: Well, no. They'll distract you from looking for your way.

Director: But don't they pay attention to you?

Friend: I suppose they do.

Director: Then how good is it if you're ignoring them?

Friend: I guess it's not so good. So what do you think we should do?

Director: Learn to see with just one eye.

Friend: You mean to keep one eye out for our path and one on those we're with?

Director: Yes. If everyone did this, don't you think the world would be a better place?

Friend: I guess I do. But then again, if everyone is keeping an eye out for something else — then whose undivided attention can we claim?

JEALOUSY (ARTIST)

Artist: The only way not to be jealous of someone walking with destiny is to walk with destiny yourself.

Director: Profound words from one who I've heard many times claim to have no destiny of his own.

Artist: As you full well know, my works have destinies.

Director: Then let me ask you the hard question, Artist. And I'm asking sincerely. Are you jealous of your works?

Artist: Ha! You're the first one to ask me that.

Director: Well?

Artist: In truth? Sometimes I am.

Director: So why not have your own destiny?

Artist: Because I channel all my energy into my works.

Director: You might be selling yourself short.

Artist: Really? If my jealousy gnawed at me day and night, I might agree with you, my friend. But when I'm at work, I feel nothing but the joy of my work.

Director: It's only when you relax that you feel jealous?

Artist: Yes.

Director: Then do you try to never relax?

Artist: No, I try to find ways to relax without jealousy. And, Director, I find these ways with you!

Director: You find talking with me to be soothing?

Artist: Oh, most definitely.

Director: Why?

Artist: Because I have nothing to be jealous of in you.

Opportunities (Scientist)

Scientist: It's simple. If you can't see your opportunities you can't see your destiny.

Director: And if you can't act on your opportunities you can't live your destiny?

Scientist: Yes.

Director: How do we see our opportunities?

Scientist: We need to study our surroundings, our environment.

Director: And if we study, the opportunities will just become obvious?

Scientist: Well, you have to study with an eye to opportunity.

Director: How does that differ from simply studying, studying the way a scientist would?

Scientist: When you simply study you're more objective.

Director: Because you don't put yourself in the picture?

Scientist: Right.

Director: But don't you want to be objective when it comes to your opportunities?

Scientist: I'm afraid that's not possible. All opportunity is subjective.

Director: Until you act on it?

Scientist: Yes, and that's a profound insight.

Director: I'm not sure about that. But what changes when you act on your opportunity?

Scientist: It's no longer an opportunity. It's a fact.

Director: Is it a fact if you act on your opportunity but fail?

Scientist: Both successes and failures are facts.

Director: So is it best for opportunity to become a fact, no matter what kind?

Scientist: Than never to become a fact at all? Better to fail than to never have tried.

Director: Then may we succeed. But if we fail, then may we have the courage to take pride in our attempt — and to look once more for where opportunity and destiny meet.

Attraction (Friend)

Friend: Do those you're attracted to always lead you to your destiny?

Director: Yes — provided you know when to keep away from them.

Friend: How would I know?

Director: How else? You have to talk to them.

Friend: And ask them what?

Director: How will you lead me to my destiny? Based on their answer, you'll know.

Friend: Oh, but be serious! I can't ask them that. They'll think I'm crazy!

Director: Would you think they're crazy if they asked you?

Friend: Well, I would think it a little odd.

Director: Really, Friend — what's so odd about asking a question as important as that? Wouldn't it be more odd if you never asked that question at all?

Friend: You have a point. But I think it's something you ask yourself, not the other.

Director: Fair enough. But we may have been hasty in our formulation of the question.

Friend: How so?

Director: Shouldn't the question be: How will having you in my life help me walk my destined path? Do you see the difference?

Friend: Of course I do. The first question implies you don't yet know your destiny and need to be led to it. The second implies you know but could use some help along the way. So are you saying we need to know our destiny first, before we follow our attractions?

Director: Well, we'll almost certainly follow some attractions before we know our destiny. So maybe the first version of the question isn't all that bad. But as we gain in experience and learn our way, we'll adopt the revised question. And then beyond these questions there's a third I think we'll need to ask, if we really want to know what we should do.

Friend: What question is that?

Director: How will I help you?

USEFUL (ARTIST)

Artist: We all want to feel useful.

Director: Useful as in we have a purpose?

Artist: Yes.

Director: Have a purpose as in we have a destiny?

Artist: Sure.

Director: Then we all want to have a destiny.

Artist: Ha! You say it as if we arrived here through a difficult stretch of reasoning.

Director: Even if we didn't, does that make it any less true, if it's true?

Artist: No. But you know I don't want to have a destiny.

Director: Yes, I know. But you want it for your work. So let's consider your work. Do you want your work to be useful?

Artist: Of course. And yes, all the rest applies. Purpose. Destiny.

Director: Okay. But what's useful about your work?

Artist: It gives others a sense of purpose and spurs them on.

Director: But couldn't you do that yourself, without your art?

Artist: No, I couldn't.

Director: Why not?

Artist: I can never see what I can say to help until it's far too late.

Director: And you put the things you should have said into your work?

Artist: Yes. It's the only way I can be of use.

Director: But doesn't being useful give you purpose? And if purpose....

Artist: Yes, yes. I have use and purpose — but no destiny. It's like I always try to tell you. When I'm done with it, my work lives on its own. And then I, in a way, am dead. There is no destiny for the dead, my friend. So I don't work for destiny. I try to find a way to live.

Trapped (Scientist)

Scientist: Can we feel trapped in our destiny?

Director: Yes, but can't that be good?

Scientist: How?

Director: You feel you have no choice but to live your destiny.

Scientist: Yes, but if you feel you have no choice, do you really deserve credit?

Director: Scientist, don't you know that destiny isn't about credit?

Scientist: What's it about?

Director: It's only about itself.

Scientist: What does that mean?

Director: It means destiny isn't about praise or blame. It's not about pleasure or pain. It's not about knowledge or ignorance. It's not about true or false.

Scientist: In other words, it's not about anything!

Director: Mostly it's about itself.

Scientist: But that's crazy!

Director: Why?

Scientist: Well, for one, why should you bother to live your destiny?

Director: What if it isn't a bother?

Scientist: But we were talking about feeling trapped. Feeling trapped is certainly a bother. Or wouldn't you agree?

Director: I don't know. Is it bad to feel trapped in something good?

Scientist: But weren't you just saying destiny isn't about good or bad?

Director: No, I didn't quite say that. Destiny can surely be about both good and bad.

Scientist: So if my destiny is good does that mean I ought to lock myself into my way? But where is my freedom then? And if I'm no longer free — then what am I?

CONTRADICTION (FRIEND)

Friend: I don't think destiny requires perfect consistency.

Director: Sometimes we need to contradict ourselves in order to move forward?

Friend: Yes.

Director: Why are people afraid to contradict themselves?

Friend: Because I suppose they feel their words have the force of an oath.

Director: So if I tell you my favorite flavor of ice cream is vanilla, but then I tell someone else my favorite flavor is cashew chocolate double chunk with cookie dough — I've broken my oath?

Friend: Well, yes.

Director: But what if I was speaking truth in either case? Sometimes vanilla is my favorite. And sometimes cashew chocolate double chunk with cookie dough is.

Friend: Then that's what you should say. But people often want you to have only one favorite.

Director: Why?

Friend: I don't know. I just know it's true — and more so when it comes to the more important things.

Director: What sort of more important things?

Friend: Destiny, for one. They want to know if you believe in it, and they don't want you to keep changing your mind.

Director: But I don't understand why what I believe is so important to them. And is it really about my belief? Couldn't I be consistent in belief but merely change what I say?

Friend: That's even worse. Then in addition to contradicting yourself you're telling a lie. But why is all of this so important to them? Maybe they're tempted to contradict themselves — and fear your example might lead them astray.

Director: But what are you saying? If they're so tempted, doesn't that mean there wasn't full truth in what they already said? They want to have less than full truth? Fine. Then it's one flavor and only one flavor for them — no matter what they might crave.

Duty (Artist)

Artist: Sometimes duty is destiny.

Director: And sometimes duty breaks us?

Artist: Yes, and that too can be destiny.

Director: But when it doesn't break us?

Artist: It makes us strong.

Director: What sort of duty do you live by, Artist?

Artist: The duty to create my works.

Director: Does that duty ever break you?

Artist: Each and every time!

Director: What exactly does it break?

Artist: My heart.

Director: But why?

Artist: Because all my works go on without me.

Director: Can't you travel along with them?

Artist: They're better off alone.

Director: But don't you have a duty to support your works?

Artist: My personal flaws would only detract from what I've made.

Director: Couldn't you at least interpret your art for those who don't know how?

Artist: And ruin the fun? No. Look, Director. I'll keep on my broken hearted way because it's the price I pay for what I do. But I'll let you in on a secret. The kind of broken heart I have is rare — because every now and then it overwhelms me with feeling... sweet! Sweet that my art gives pleasure to others. Sweet that some of them will understand the meaning of my works. Sweet that both my works and some of these others will live on and on beyond me. So the broken heart, it's not so bad. Because sometimes it makes me feel whole and free.

Significance (Scientist)

Scientist: Destiny never feels insignificant to the destined.

Director: Why not?

Scientist: Because how else would you know it's destiny?

Director: That's like saying hot peppers never feel insignificant to the eater.

Scientist: Why wouldn't they?

Director: Because how else would you know they're hot?

Scientist: But that's a ridiculous example.

Director: Shall we try to think up a better one?

Scientist: No. I want to know why you think destiny might feel insignificant.

Director: But I don't think that.

Scientist: Then what makes destiny feel significant?

Director: I suppose it's when things start making sense.

Scientist: What do you mean by that?

Director: All the little things you do, all the little things that are done to you — they all tend toward a certain end.

Scientist: The end of your destiny.

Director: Yes.

Scientist: But what about the big things you do, and the big things that are done to you?

Director: The little things will give you the confidence you need for bigger things. After all, what are bigger things but lots of little things rolled into one?

Scientist: I'm not so sure that's always true. But I take the general point.

Director: Good. So when you start to feel the significance of destiny, what must you do?

Scientist: You must go on and on with it and never stop. No matter how hot your tongue!

Distractions (Friend)

Friend: Sometimes distractions from destiny are good.

Director: They refresh us?

Friend: Yes.

Director: They make us ready for another go?

Friend: Exactly.

Director: And sometimes we get lost in them?

Friend: Yes, I think that's true.

Director: How do we find our way back out?

Friend: I'm not sure we always do.

Director: What happens to those who are hopelessly lost in distractions?

Friend: I think at first they seem to thrive.

Director: Thrive? Really?

Friend: Yes. The distractions are fresh and new. And if the person is young, or young at heart, he or she appears to be doing very well in them.

Director: But we know there's a rottenness growing inside?

Friend: We do. Any time you're away from your destiny for long you start to decay.

Director: But can't we see this happening to ourselves?

Friend: I don't think most people can — until it's too late.

Director: Too late?

Friend: Your destiny won't have you back.

Director: But do you really think that happens? Your destiny turning you away? If it's truly your destiny, won't it always be there for you when you return?

Friend: Maybe, Director. Maybe. But the longer you're away, the harder it will be to reunite. And even then, your destiny will almost certainly no longer be what it once was.

SIMPLICITY (ARTIST)

Artist: The greatest art is simple.

Director: Just as is the greatest destiny?

Artist: Oh, I don't know. Destinies can be very complex.

Director: Yes, but can they be complex and great?

Artist: What do you think?

Director: I'm inclined to think the simpler the greater. There's less to get in the way.

Artist: But what if you feel your destiny is in fact complex?

Director: You have to find a way to simplify.

Artist: Yes, but not at the cost of the nuance and subtlety in your life.

Director: Right. And just look at your art. It's simple yet has subtlety and nuance. So what do you think? Would you prefer a simple destiny?

Artist: I would, if I ever wanted a destiny.

Director: And would you prefer a simple destiny for your works?

Artist: That's where I have to say no. The height of success is for a simple work to have a complex destiny.

Director: I've never understood why you artists think that's true.

Artist: I give one answer you don't like and now I'm 'you artists'? But what if I tell you it simply can't be helped?

Director: Why not?

Artist: Because the work, even a very simple work, affects different people differently.

Director: Then why isn't the destiny of every work complex?

Artist: Because some works don't speak to many different types of people — even if they reach millions. These millions can all be by and large the same in their opinions and beliefs. But other works, though reaching fewer numbers, speak to a broader range of human types. And so the overall effect is necessarily complex.

Depression (Scientist)

Scientist: Have you ever been depressed?

Director: Aren't we all depressed from time to time, Scientist?

Scientist: Yes, but I'm talking about real depression, deep depression.

Director: Why do you ask?

Scientist: Because I'm wondering if being depressed necessarily means you're not following your destiny.

Director: Oh, I don't think it does.

Scientist: Can you give an example of when it doesn't?

Director: Sure. Suppose that while we're on our way we have to go through a difficult change, a metamorphosis. This might cause our spirits to sink. But we're still on our way — just in a very rough patch.

Scientist: Okay. But let's suppose we're not on our way, Director. Could that depress us?

Director: Yes, of course.

Scientist: Would the depression be our fault?

Director: Not if we're not on our way because it's impossible for us to be on our way.

Scientist: Well, that's the question, then. Is it always possible to be on our way?

Director: Well.... In some way, shape, or form? I think it is. But 'possible' covers a lot of ground. The possible can be excruciatingly hard.

Scientist: So even if it's all but impossible to follow our destiny, and we don't, we're at fault for any depression that ensues?

Director: Ensues from that specific cause, yes. But I don't like to say it.

Scientist: What's this? Why not?

Director: Because it seems hard to blame someone for not doing the next to impossible.

Scientist: Not when you ask that much of yourself.

THE MOMENTS (FRIEND)

Friend: I think too much 'living in the moment' can make you lose sight of your destiny.

Director: That's funny. I thought living in the moment is the key to destiny.

Friend: How do you mean?

Director: Well, what does it mean to live in the moment?

Friend: To forget about anything but what you're doing at the time.

Director: What else could you be thinking about other than what you're doing at the time?

Friend: Your future.

Director: And that's the opposite of the here and now? That's the there and then?

Friend: You could put it that way.

Director: And the past, that's also the there and then, isn't it?

Friend: True.

Director: Now, to have a good destiny, would you say we need to be rooted in the past?

Friend: Of course.

Director: And, similarly, I take it, we have to keep an eye to the future. But we can't be blind to the present, right?

Friend: No doubt.

Director: So here's the thing. Would you believe me if I told you the here and now is the bridge to the there and then? I mean, without the present, some sort of present, is there a future or even a past? Do you know what I mean?

Friend: I do. And now I understand why you say living in the moment is the key to destiny. But I'd make one small change.

Director: Oh? What?

Friend: We have to live not just in the moment, but the moments, all of the moments — past, present, and future, too — at once. Awake to them all, we travel destiny's way.

Promises (Artist)

Artist: There's an art in knowing when to promise.

Director: Oh?

Artist: Well, actually, it's more of a rule.

Director: But you don't like to follow rules.

Artist: And who says I like to promise? But here it is anyway, Director. The only time to promise is when holding yourself to your word amounts to holding yourself to your destiny.

Director: So if you think your destiny is to always keep your word, you'll have a greater destiny if you make promises all the time?

Artist: I knew I could count on you to try to make this ridiculous.

Director: Sorry, Artist. But isn't that a problem with your rule?

Artist: There are people who think it's their destiny to merely keep their word. And some of them are weak. So when they're pressed, which happens often, out pops a promise.

Director: And some of these promises aren't good for them to keep?

Artist: Absolutely not. They were promises made under duress.

Director: What's better? To keep a bad promise or to break it?

Artist: You know these people. They'd die of guilt for breaking any promise, even one that's forced from them.

Director: So it's better never to make the promise in the first place?

Artist: Yes, of course. And it's better for them not to conceive of their destiny as filled with nothing more than promises.

Director: How should they conceive of their destiny?

Artist: That's a big question with no general answer.

Director: Here's a general answer. They should think of it as what's good for them. And then only give their word toward that end.

Keys (Scientist)

Scientist: Destiny is forward facing.

Director: But don't we all need to look back from time to time?

Scientist: Of course. But we shouldn't derive our destiny solely from our past.

Director: When should we look to the past?

Scientist: When the past holds a key.

Director: A key to the future?

Scientist: Yes, but also a key to the present.

Director: How will we know we have the key?

Scientist: Possibilities will open up before us.

Director: Destiny is about possibilities?

Scientist: Of course. What else would it be about?

Director: The way.

Scientist: Yes, but I don't think it's always that simple.

Director: Why not?

Scientist: There can be more than one way.

Director: And we can find the keys to those ways through looking to the past? In other words, the past can hold more than one key?

Scientist: Often times? Yes.

Director: So let's suppose we find a key, but it doesn't open one of our ways. What does that mean?

Scientist: It means we've found someone else's key. And now it's part of our destiny to find out whose it is.

Director: And if we find the person and they open their door?

Scientist: There's a chance, if we walk through with them, we'll find a key of our own.

COMPETITION (FRIEND)

Friend: Destiny should never be a matter of competition. Yes, you might compete for an honor and so on. But it should never be about the actual competition, the winning.

Director: Why?

Friend: Because it's about what you do, how you do it.

Director: You can lose the race and still win a great destiny?

Friend: Yes.

Director: All because of the way you handled yourself during the race?

Friend: That's right.

Director: And might it also be because of the things you do when you're off the track, so to speak?

Friend: It's especially because of those things.

Director: The off-the-track things are never about winning, are they?

Friend: Well, there's training for a win. But in broader terms? No, they're not.

Director: Do you think they're more important than an actual win?

Friend: I do.

Director: Why doesn't everyone see it this way?

Friend: They have winning fever.

Director: You mean winning is all they can think about?

Friend: That's right.

Director: But isn't it sometimes very important to win? Like in a war, for instance.

Friend: Yes, of course. It's crucial to win in war.

Director: Is winning the war more important than the off-the-track things?

Friend: No, because what's the point to winning without them?

FORCING IT (ARTIST)

Artist: No good art is forced.

Director: It has to come gently? But haven't you heard people say that creating works of art is like giving birth?

Artist: Of course I've heard that. That's how it is for some. But not for me.

Director: Creation comes easily to you?

Artist: I wouldn't say it comes easily. But I would say my creations come out of me without my uttering a cry.

Director: But the creation itself, does it cry?

Artist: Of course it does! That's how it starts to make its way in the world.

Director: How do you think all this applies to destiny?

Artist: It's the same sort of thing.

Director: Can you say more?

Artist: Sure. Some people's way is filled with moans, groans, screams, and cries — and all of it for a mediocre destiny at best! But others go quietly and gently about their way and make a great destiny without causing so much as a fuss.

Director: What do you think accounts for the difference?

Artist: I've often wondered. And here's what I conclude. The former type, the noisy ones, they over-reach. They're trying to make their destiny more than what it is.

Director: And the gentle ones know their destiny for what it is?

Artist: Not always. But they have more courage in trying to find it out and then in doing what must be done.

Director: How so?

Artist: They're willing to learn and act on their own. And we see it in this. Every scream and shout by the noisy ones says, in effect, Come help me find my way! And that's even though they like to think they know their way! They want to force the issue. But the gentle know that can't be done. And so destiny, no lover of being coerced, is theirs.

SPREADING THE WORD (SCIENTIST)

Scientist: Sometimes I get so overwhelmed.

Director: By what?

Scientist: By all the speaking invitations I receive.

Director: Why do they overwhelm you?

Scientist: Because I have to spend time preparing, then I have to travel, then I have to get familiar enough with the venue, then I have to deliver my lecture, then I have to take questions, then I have to mingle afterwards, then I have to go out to dinner with the sponsors, then I have to travel back, and then I'm exhausted!

Director: So why do you do it?

Scientist: It's expected of me.

Director: You'd be rude to refuse?

Scientist: In so many words? Yes.

Director: But this takes you away from your work.

Scientist: That's true... in a way.

Director: In a way?

Scientist: Spreading the word about my work is also part of my work, my way.

Director: Why?

Scientist: What do you mean?

Director: Can't your work speak for itself?

Scientist: Well, yes — I suppose that's true.

Director: Then why not let it speak and free yourself to do more work?

Scientist: Because I want to talk about the implications of my work.

Director: You mean you want to help steer where people go with it?

Scientist: Yes. And who better to co-pilot than the one who built the plane?

Regret (Friend)

Friend: Regrets are best used as fuel for our future.

Director: I'm not sure I understand.

Friend: When you feel regret, what can you do?

Director: Make up for it?

Friend: Yes. And don't you feel that as a drive? And if you feel it as a drive, can't it be used to propel you into the future?

Director: You may have a point. But what happens when you run out of fuel?

Friend: You mean you feel no regrets? But do we ever really feel no regrets?

Director: I'm inclined to think it's possible. So I think we need a better fuel.

Friend: Like what?

Director: Desire.

Friend: Yes, but desire won't always last.

Director: Why not?

Friend: Well, what kind of desire are you talking about?

Director: Oh, just the standard sort of desire. A strong feeling of want.

Friend: But we often want one thing one day and something else another.

Director: Not if we want the one thing badly enough.

Friend: Alright. But isn't desire the cousin of regret?

Director: Why would you say that?

Friend: Because most desire goes unfulfilled. And then it becomes regret.

Director: But that assumes we think there was something we could have done to fulfill our desire, that we somehow fell short, that it could have been ours.

Friend: Yes, and that's exactly what we think.

HEARTLESS (ARTIST)

Artist: Just because you're heartless doesn't mean you can't have a destiny.

Director: Really? What kind of destiny can you have?

Artist: It depends on who you make as friends.

Director: Friends? What kind of friends can the heartless have?

Artist: Oh, you'd be surprised.

Director: Do the friends of the heartless have hearts?

Artist: Mostly? No. But there are some....

Director: Some?

Artist: Some with hearts who don't want to believe the heartless haven't got hearts.

Director: Why don't they want to believe it?

Artist: Because it's important to them to believe everyone has a heart.

Director: It's simply their way of looking at the world?

Artist: Yes.

Director: Do you think they're wrong?

Artist: Of course I do!

Director: How can you persuade them?

Artist: Bah, there's no way with these people. But that's what makes them work their part in the destiny of the heartless.

Director: How so?

Artist: It turns out the heartless do have something like a heart, but not a heart, buried somewhere deep inside. The believers in heart have the ability to find this thing and break it — all the while thinking they've found and have nurtured the heart.

Director: Who knew belief could have such force?

Artist: Certainly not the heartless — until it's too late.

INSIGHT (SCIENTIST)

Scientist: You don't need perfect health in order to walk with destiny.

Director: Why not?

Scientist: Because the afflicted often have insights that the rest of us lack. And destiny loves insight.

Director: What is an insight?

Scientist: What do you mean?

Director: I mean what does it mean to have an insight into something? Does it mean you grasp the secret workings of the thing?

Scientist: I think it does.

Director: So the afflicted grasp the secret workings of things?

Scientist: Yes.

Director: What things?

Scientist: Well, think of the blind. Don't you think they know things about the secret workings of hearing that those with sight don't know?

Director: I suppose that's often true. And I take it you'd say the same about the deaf?

Scientist: I would. They know things about sight that those with hearing don't.

Director: Can the deaf and blind walk with destiny without these insights?

Scientist: No. These insights open their way.

Director: I wonder. Is it possible for someone with sight and hearing to gain the same insight into hearing and sight that the blind and deaf so often have?

Scientist: The same insight? I'm not so sure.

Director: Why?

Scientist: Honestly? Well, I'm somewhat embarrassed to say. It's because it wouldn't seem... fair.

PARALLELS (FRIEND)

Friend: I believe there are people with parallel destinies.

Director: And do you believe there are people who are on the exact same track?

Friend: If there are, that's a problem.

Director: Why?

Friend: Because then one of them is following the other's destiny.

Director: Instead of following their own?

Friend: Yes.

Director: But can't we have that problem with parallel destinies? Can't each follow the other's lead?

Friend: You mean they coordinate their lives in order to stay in parallel?

Director: Yes. Do you think that's good?

Friend: Only if their destinies are truly meant to influence each other that way.

Director: And if they're not? And they still coordinate their lives? Why would they?

Friend: They probably don't like to be alone.

Director: And so they travel together in parallel.

Friend: Oh, but it's not really that. They're constantly pulling together and pushing apart.

Director: While parallels that are meant to be stay constantly aligned?

Friend: Yes. And they feel they're exactly where they need to be.

Director: Is this true even if they can't see each other?

Friend: What do you mean?

Director: I mean some parallels are very far apart.

Friend: Then how do they know they're aligned?

Director: They simply trust the way.

LIFE'S WORK (ARTIST)

Artist: Yes, I have a life's work.

Director: What does that mean? That you simply work for most of your life on your art, or do you mean something else?

Artist: I mean something else. I mean there are themes that run through and unify all my individual works.

Director: What are those themes?

Artist: Ha! That's for me to know and you to find out.

Director: But suppose I found out, and came to you and told you about them — would you confirm them for me then?

Artist: If you really understood my works? I'm not sure.

Director: Why not?

Artist: Because I can't have you running around telling everyone what my work is all about.

Director: What harm is there in that?

Artist: Some of the themes are controversial.

Director: You don't want to be known as a controversial artist?

Artist: I want to be left alone. And controversy is the last thing I need.

Director: Has anyone ever figured out your themes?

Artist: All of them? No. Sure, they see the obvious ones. But there are many more I keep submerged.

Director: Submerged?

Artist: You know — below the surface.

Director: So you want your audience to dive deep into your works?

Artist: What artist worth their salt would have it any other way?

COMPROMISES (SCIENTIST)

Scientist: We all must compromise at times.

Director: Even those of us who feel we have destinies?

Scientist: Yes, even so. But when it comes to destiny, we never compromise in the center, only on the periphery.

Director: Can you give me an example, Scientist, of what you mean by center and periphery?

Scientist: Of course. In my case, scientific work is the center. And securing funding is on the periphery.

Director: But it seems to me that the periphery, in your case, is the lifeblood of the center. No?

Scientist: Well, yes, in a sense that's true.

Director: So if you want to perform experiment X, scientific work in the center, but the ones with the money are only interested in experiment Z — don't you have no choice but to compromise the core and go with Z?

Scientist: You're asking if a compromise in the periphery necessarily leads to a compromise in the center?

Director: Yes. I mean, shouldn't you only take money for X if X is what you really want to do?

Scientist: True. But sometimes you have to work your way to what you want to do. You start with Z. And if you have success, you move to Y. And if again you have success, there's a good chance you'll find funding for X. That's really not a compromise. It's only being smart. But that's enough about me. What about you? I've heard you say philosophy is the center of your life.

Director: Yes. But unlike you I often compromise. But never in my core.

Scientist: You compromise in the periphery? Tell me how.

Director: I compromise with those who care nothing for philosophy. I can't share my love for it with them. And so I temporize while I look for others who appreciate the central part of me.

TREADMILL (FRIEND)

Friend: Does destiny ever feel like you're running on a treadmill?

Director: You mean you're trying hard but getting nowhere?

Friend: Yes.

Director: No, I don't think destiny feels like that. Is that how you feel?

Friend: It is.

Director: Hmm.

Friend: Hmm what?

Director: You need to feel like you're getting somewhere.

Friend: Thanks for the insight.

Director: But do you know how you might be able to feel that way?

Friend: Tell me.

Director: Get off the treadmill and walk.

Friend: Walk where?

Director: Outdoors.

Friend: And that will make me feel I'm walking with destiny?

Director: I'm not sure.

Friend: Then why would you tell me to do it?

Director: Because I think it's good to enjoy fresh air. And who knows? Maybe you'll find your way while you're out there.

Friend: Is that the secret, then? Do what you enjoy and you might find your way?

Director: I didn't know it was a secret. So will you try it?

Friend: Yes, of course.

Director: Then let me wish you luck.

Outside (Artist)

Artist: We all need examples to follow, examples of those who made their own destiny. But maybe 'follow' is the wrong word. We just need to know what's possible. And it doesn't hurt if the example comes from a field different than our own.

Director: When you say 'we', Artist — are you including yourself?

Artist: Of course not.

Director: So what you're really saying is that 'people' all need examples to follow, and so on, and so on.

Artist: Did you ever have any doubt that's what I meant?

Director: I did, for a moment. But do you know what I'm most curious about?

Artist: Of course I do. You're intrigued by my mention of examples that come from a field other than your own.

Director: How did you know that?

Artist: Because learning what's possible inside your field, from those outside your field, makes you something of an outsider.

Director: But what does that mean?

Artist: You know what it means. It means you're different.

Director: And different is good?

Artist: Different is great! So long as you're strong enough to take the strain.

Director: The strain of being often outside?

Artist: Of course! You're out there in the elements. You don't think that causes strain? But I'll tell you of another strain you'll face. The ones inside will compare themselves to you.

Director: Because they suspect it takes strength to stand outside?

Artist: Yes. And how many of them will prove to be as strong, having lived inside so long? They'll hate you for your strength.

Director: Then we must find the ones who don't.

Shorter Ways (Scientist)

Scientist: Director, do you believe people can take shortcuts to their destiny?

Director: I don't see how they could. Their ways are their ways. No?

Scientist: Maybe 'shortcut' is the wrong word. What if we're talking about a shorter way, a real way, that truly leads to the same place as taking the long way round?

Director: Hmm. The end might be the same, but what about everything else along the way?

Scientist: There will be a different 'everything else', that's all.

Director: A different everything else seems a lot like a different destiny to me. But let's not get caught up on that. You're saying it's simply a different and better way?

Scientist: Precisely. It's more efficient.

Director: You mean it's not a winding road.

Scientist: Yes.

Director: But if we're going to end up in the same place, why should we rush?

Scientist: Who says we'd have to rush? We can go more slowly when we take the more efficient route and get there at the same time.

Director: Hmm. This sounds more promising than at first. But with the winding road you see more things along the way. No?

Scientist: If you have to hurry to get to the end, then what can you truly see?

Director: That's a fair point. So how do I find my shorter way?

Scientist: You just need to know the end and then map your way out along as straight a line as you can.

Director: Ah, but that's just it! How do I know the end?

Scientist: What do you mean? The end is simply where you want to be.

Director: But, Scientist, what if I want to be where I am?

Scientist: Then I guess you've found the shortest route there is.

LEGACY (FRIEND)

Friend: A destiny doesn't have to involve some great big legacy.

Director: What might it involve?

Friend: The legacy of a kind smile at just the right time.

Director: Yes. But would it be more of a legacy if you gave more than one kind smile at just the right time?

Friend: Well, yes, I suppose.

Director: Would it be more of a legacy still if in addition to smiles you had kind words?

Friend: I guess.

Director: Tell me. If you had to choose between a smile and a word, which would it be?

Friend: Oh, but that's an impossible choice!

Director: Why?

Friend: Because one might fit one set of circumstances and the other another.

Director: So if you want to leave a legacy, you need to understand these things?

Friend: Yes, of course.

Director: And that's so no matter how great the legacy?

Friend: I think that's true. Don't you?

Director: I do. But tell me this. If you wish to leave a great big legacy, is the set of circumstances you must master greater and more difficult than what you'd have to master in order to leave a little legacy?

Friend: But what's a 'great big legacy'? A great many words? A great many smiles? Or do we mean lots of money, lots of fame, and so on? And who says a big legacy is better than a little legacy? Each legacy is unique. So how can we possibly judge?

Director: You have a point. So if we want to leave a legacy, of whatever sort, what must we do?

Friend: Just focus on our destiny, and let the legacy take care of itself.

CHANCE (ARTIST)

Artist: Is there a degree of chance in the fact that I'm good at my art? Of course! In fact, there might be more than a degree.

Director: What's more than a degree?

Artist: The whole thing. Total chance.

Director: You'd say that about yourself? Your skill is just due to luck?

Artist Yes, I would say that. But now you should ask me about destiny.

Director: You're not going to say that destiny is total chance.

Artist: Oh, yes I am.

Director: But why?

Artist: Because I'm saving destiny from its opposite.

Director: What opposite?

Artist: That everything is determined, is fixed with no way out. At least with the free play of chance we can have some fun.

Director: But what's the difference? In either case there's no free will. We can't control chance any more than we can control when everything is fixed.

Artist: Ah, yes! You've put your finger right on it, my friend. There is no difference between the two.

Director: You look triumphant.

Artist: It's because we're speaking truth.

Director: But then how can we say the play of chance is fun?

Artist: You're asking because we can't tell it from its opposite?

Director: Yes. We might as well say that when everything is absolutely fixed it's time to have some fun.

Artist: And it is! But I know, I know. It's all a question of perspective. And, for many, 'fixed fun' will simply never ring true.

GOODNESS (SCIENTIST)

Scientist: Goodness in no way guarantees the destiny you want.

Director: But how can you say that, Scientist?

Scientist: From long experience, Director.

Director: Long experience of being good? So you're not satisfied with your destiny?

Scientist: The periphery is encroaching on the center, if you know what I mean.

Director: Yes, I think I do. But....

Scientist: But what?

Director: But how do you know you've been good?

Scientist: What are you saying?

Director: I'm saying maybe it's true that goodness does guarantee the destiny you want.

Scientist: Well, I know I've been good.

Director: Do you have any independent verification?

Scientist: You mean like a review by my peers? Of course I don't.

Director: Why not?

Scientist: Because who can truly say who's been good?

Director: Oh, I think we can say. After all, you said it about yourself.

Scientist: Yes, but I know myself.

Director: Not all of us do.

Scientist: That's very true. And when we don't we can't know others, either.

Director: Do you see others who are bad who are happy with their lot?

Scientist: In truth? Yes. But I don't believe badness was the cause. Badness doesn't guarantee the destiny you want.

Director: Well, if it doesn't matter either way — then I think you might as well be good.

Advantage (Friend)

Friend: Do you think it's fair to take advantage in order to secure your destiny?

Director: Take advantage? Take advantage of what?

Friend: Of people.

Director: No, Friend, I don't think that's fair.

Friend: But what if we make a distinction?

Director: Between what?

Friend: On the one hand we can take advantage of people. On the other hand we can take advantage of situations.

Director: And you think the latter are fair game, not the former?

Friend: What do you think?

Director: I think people are intricately tied to situations.

Friend: So to take advantage of situations is to take advantage of people?

Director: That's how it seems to me. So would you do it?

Friend: No.

Director: Why?

Friend: Because as you said, it isn't fair!

Director: Yes, but would you rather give the advantage to others?

Friend: Honestly? I think I would.

Director: And that would be fair?

Friend: To me? Well, no. But maybe there's another way.

Director: A neutral path to tread?

Friend: Yes. Give no advantage, take no advantage. What do you think?

Director: I think to walk that way is a great deal harder than it seems.

HESITATION (ARTIST)

Artist: Truly great artists never hesitate in their work.

Director: They rush right in?

Artist: No, of course not.

Director: Then what do they do?

Artist: First they see everything in one strike of the eye.

Director: And when they have?

Artist: Then they know what needs to be done.

Director: And what of those who hesitate?

Artist: They'll never be great.

Director: Even if it's only a little hesitation?

Artist: Even so.

Director: That seems like an awfully high standard to set.

Artist: What can I say? Art is no easy affair.

Director: Can artists learn not to hesitate if they don't know how?

Artist: That's a difficult thing.

Director: What does it involve?

Artist: Another strike of the eye.

Director: On what?

Artist: The things that make you hesitate. You must see them all in one look. Then you'll know what needs to be done.

Director: Can you see and know but fail to act?

Artist: Of course. But if you fail to act often enough? Well, then you'll no longer be able to see.

All In (Scientist)

Scientist: We must give everything we've got. What other choice do we have? To follow a destiny of 'could have' and 'should have'? That amounts to nothing in the end.

Director: But what if we give everything we've got — to the wrong thing?

Scientist: What do you mean?

Director: I mean what if we need to step back a bit and have a look around before committing all of our resources, internal and external both?

Scientist: Step back in order to see what else there is in life?

Director: Yes.

Scientist: Well, you have a point, of course. But we can do that when we rest.

Director: If what you're saying is literally true, and we're giving all we've got, how often do we truly rest?

Scientist: Well, not as often as we should.

Director: And what's the quality of the rest?

Scientist: Blacked out exhaustion.

Director: Are we doing much looking around then? And even if we do manage to look around, how much energy will we have to devote to curiosity?

Scientist: You mean to following up on what we're curious about? To really explore?

Director: Yes. Don't you think the greatest destinies are for those who explore most?

Scientist: I do.

Director: Then before going all in, as they say, we should make sure we've let our curiosity take us through all the interesting possibilities first. No?

Scientist: But, Director, there are endless possibilities! We could spend a lifetime exploring without finding that one thing, the thing to which we want to sacrifice our all, to give everything we've got.

Director: Yes, that may be. But isn't there joy in exploration? And what better in life than joy? I would have thought you of all people could appreciate this.

Respect (Friend)

Friend: Some people think their destiny is to be respected. But I think they'll find that's a hollow destiny unless they qualify it by saying respected by whom.

Director: I think that's a very good point. So whose respect do you want?

Friend: Well, yours for one.

Director: You've got it. Whose else?

Friend: Anyone that I respect — my friends especially.

Director: You don't want the respect of those you don't respect?

Friend: Why would I?

Director: Because they might harm you.

Friend: By not respecting me?

Director: Look at it this way. If an enemy doesn't respect you, what happens?

Friend: You're in danger of attack.

Director: But if an enemy respects you?

Friend: He or she will think twice about attack.

Director: And what about the other way round? Should you respect your enemies?

Friend: You mean so I don't do anything foolish toward them? Yes, I suppose I should.

Director: Then how strange this all seems. You want everyone's respect, friends and enemies both. And you respect your friends and enemies both.

Friend: But who can have respect from all and give respect to all?

Director: Well, no one, I suppose. So it seems there's something of a choice.

Friend: I choose respect with friends.

Director: Why?

Friend: Because I'd rather do foolish things and be attacked than lose an ounce of love.

Followers (Artist)

Artist: Here's the dilemma. Can tyrants who follow their own destiny feel good about followers who aren't following theirs?

Director: Your question seems wrong in so many ways.

Artist: Humor me.

Director: Alright. But let's forget about the tyrant feeling good and focus on the followers. There are two types. Those who in following a tyrant follow their own destiny — and we can call these true followers. And those who in following a tyrant betray their own destiny — and we can call these false followers. Does that make sense?

Artist: Yes.

Director: Which type of follower is it best for a tyrant to have?

Artist: Well, here's the funny thing. It's best to have the false.

Director: Why?

Artist: Because the true followers are weak. And the false followers are strong — or at least they're potentially strong.

Director: 'Potentially strong' because they'd grow stronger if they broke away and followed their own independent destiny?

Artist: Yes. And that's why it's crucial for the tyrant to keep them following as long as possible. When they're independent they're a threat.

Director: Tell me. What's the biggest threat? When someone starts out as a false follower and then breaks away or when they never follow at all?

Artist: When they never follow. To do that you must be incredibly strong. And strength is a threat. So in never following you would have to live under a constant fear of attack.

Director: What must you do when you're under such a threat?

Artist: You must be wise. You must conceal the fact that you're not following along and quietly let yourself grow as strong as you can — until it's time to openly resist. And when you resist your example might encourage the false followers to set themselves free. And then general rebellion is possible. But, of course, not all the false followers will set themselves free. Which means there's a good chance you'll be crushed.

STATESMEN (SCIENTIST)

Scientist: The goal of statesmen is always the same — to make their nation's destiny their own.

Director: Why don't you say 'statespersons'? Do you have some sort of bias, Scientist?

Scientist: Ha, ha. No bias. Statespersons is just too clumsy.

Director: Alright. But what kind of destiny are you talking about? Don't even tyrants try to make their nation's destiny their own?

Scientist: Yes, I suppose they do.

Director: So why don't we ask — what's a nation?

Scientist: Ultimately? Its citizens.

Director: Do tyrants care about the citizens? Are the citizens 'their own'?

Scientist: No, I wouldn't say they are.

Director: Then tyrants have a different idea of the nation. That is, it's not the citizens.

Scientist: Yes, I think that's true.

Director: And this is the wrong idea, and because it's the wrong idea a tyrant can never be a statesman?

Scientist: Precisely. A statesman has a broader idea of the nation that he or she serves, the broadest idea of all — all of the citizens.

Director: So if you had to choose between a leader with a narrow idea of the nation and a leader with a broad idea, which would you choose?

Scientist: I would always choose the one with the broader view.

Director: Could it ever be too broad?

Scientist: How could it be too broad?

Director: I suppose a tyrant could give us an answer to that.

Scientist: Yes, but who cares what tyrants think?

EDUCATION (FRIEND)

Friend: The formal education you receive either trains you for your destiny or it doesn't. If it doesn't, then you need a strong supplement of informal education. What do you think?

Director: I think even if formal education does train you for your destiny, you still need a strong supplement of informal education. There are things that can never be formally taught, my friend.

Friend: What kind of things?

Director: Most importantly? Things that have to do with understanding people.

Friend: So let me play devil's advocate. Can't a psychology course train you in that?

Director: Yes, and so can a history course, or a philosophy course, or a number of other courses, for that matter.

Friend: Then what can't be taught?

Director: What you must do in a given situation with the understanding you have.

Friend: But can't you imagine an advanced course of study that could tell you exactly what you need to do?

Director: What you need to do according to the rules of that course of study, yes. But sometimes it takes more. You need to learn how to handle the unexpected, the things outside the bounds of any formal course.

Friend: But you can train people by putting them through unexpected scenarios.

Director: True. And that has its use. But you can't anticipate all possible series of events.

Friend: So when the wholly unanticipated happens you're saying you have nothing to fall back on but what you learned outside the bounds?

Director: Yes.

Friend: So where can I get some of this informal education?

Director: I don't know. But I've been getting some of mine from you.

REASONINGS (ARTIST)

Artist: You don't just have a destiny. You have to reason your way to it.

Director: But why can't you just have a destiny?

Artist: What? You of all people ask me that?

Director: Yes. So why not?

Artist: You're wondering if we can't just 'feel' we have a destiny?

Director: Can't we?

Artist: Is that how you know your destiny? You feel it?

Director: I feel it. But I reason about what I feel.

Artist: Why don't you feel about what you reason?

Director: I do. It goes both ways.

Artist: Ha! And when you reason about what you feel, do you change what you feel?

Director: Sometimes.

Artist: And when you feel about what you reason, do you change what you reason?

Director: I check my reasoning. And sometimes I realize I made a mistake.

Artist: But reason, in the end, is really what counts.

Director: Having good reason to feel good about my destiny is really what counts.

Artist: Then are you saying destiny is more important than reason?

Director: No, but you might find your destiny first and then find the reasons that give it support.

Artist: When you say 'find' what you mean is 'feel'?

Director: Or 'see'. But there are always reasons for what we both feel and see.

Artist: I don't know about this. I don't want reason in a mere supporting role.

Director: But if it's that or being thrown off of the stage? Which would you prefer?

Convictions (Scientist)

Scientist: A conviction is when you've reasoned as far as you can and then have to make up your mind.

Director: Really? And the further you've reasoned the greater the conviction?

Scientist: Yes.

Director: But are you suggesting that at the frontier of your convictions there might be doubt?

Scientist: At any frontier there's doubt.

Director: But how can you have made up your mind and doubt at the same time?

Scientist: You can't. But you can be aware that you've made up your mind, if you know what I mean.

Director: You mean you can be aware that what you have is opinion not knowledge.

Scientist: Precisely. Convictions are about belief.

Director: Oh. I thought you'd say convictions are about will.

Scientist: Well, they are. All belief is a sort of will.

Director: Does that mean that all beliefs are a sort of conviction?

Scientist: No, of course not. Beliefs don't need reasons. Convictions do.

Director: I'm not so sure the distinction you're drawing is true. I mean, you can have convictions that aren't backed by reason. No?

Scientist: No. It might seem that way because some people don't reason very well. But they reason to the extent they can.

Director: Okay. But how does this bear on destiny?

Scientist: The greater the convictions the greater the destiny.

Director: But 'great' doesn't necessarily mean 'good'.

Scientist: True. So let's say the better the convictions the better the destiny. And we'll stress that convictions are made better by thinking things through.

Deaf (Friend)

Friend: It's just as important to remain deaf at times as it is to listen closely.

Director: How do you know when it's time for which?

Friend: If someone is being unreasonable you have to remain deaf.

Director: And if someone is being reasonable you have to listen closely?

Friend: Yes. And there's no surer way to destiny than knowing who to listen to and not.

Director: Indeed. But how can you tell the unreasonable from the reasonable?

Friend: What do you mean?

Director: Have you ever thought someone was being unreasonable but later realized they were making sense?

Friend: Well, yes. But it was because I didn't have all the facts.

Director: The facts have the power to make the seemingly unreasonable seem reasonable?

Friend: Yes, Director. But there's also a way of speaking that tells me if someone is being reasonable.

Director: You mean they get all worked up and shout?

Friend: Of course not.

Director: Then you must mean they're calm and measured.

Friend: Exactly, yes.

Director: But couldn't someone who's calm and measured tell you untruths and lies?

Friend: I suppose.

Director: Just as someone who's all worked up could tell you truth?

Friend: I guess.

Director: So how do you know when to be deaf?

Friend: It's not so easy to say.

The Political (Artist)

Artist: The whirlwind always draws in some of the best.

Director: What whirlwind?

Artist: The political!

Director: Ah, yes. Why do you think that is?

Artist: Those who believe in their destiny beyond all sense can't resist its charm.

Director: But some who enter politics believe in their destiny with good sense. No?

Artist: In this game there is no sense.

Director: But surely there's some sense in every game.

Artist: No, it's all chaos and accidents and tumults and noise.

Director: But if that's true, wouldn't everyone with ambition know that's how it is?

Artist: Yes, yes. But they think that they can stand above the fray. They're blinded by what they take to be their destiny, the fools.

Director: Would it be better if they weren't?

Artist: You mean if they could go into it with eyes wide open?

Director: Yes. What do you think?

Artist: I think no one with eyes to see would enter politics.

Director: But we need the ones in politics to see. Right? Or is it all truly without point?

Artist: Alright, there is a point. So what do you suggest?

Director: We find those with great promise to see. And we encourage them.

Artist: Ha! And let me guess. They'll be of the noblest sort. And the more noble the blinder they'll be! But once they're in we'll help transform their souls into something great — something both seeing, wise, gentle, hard, and keen. Virtue at its best!

Director: Virtue is good. Though others will dispute with us just what virtue is.

Artist: Let them! Because our kind of virtue can prove itself, in the end.

Mentors (Scientist)

Scientist: What's the difference between those who reach their destinies with the help of mentors and those who reach them without? Nothing.

Director: Well, if you reach your destiny, you reach your destiny. There's no arguing that. But what are the odds?

Scientist: Of reaching your destiny in either case? I'm not sure.

Director: What? You don't think having a mentor improves the odds?

Scientist: It improves the odds of reaching what your mentor wants you to reach. But that's not necessarily your destiny.

Director: Are you suggesting it's best to have no mentor at all?

Scientist: I'll let you in on a secret. I had a mentor. But I didn't go with him all the way.

Director: You broke with him?

Scientist: Yes. After I had learned all I could learn.

Director: Did you feel you were somehow... dishonest?

Scientist: No! I broke with him openly and told him why.

Director: Why?

Scientist: Because he couldn't teach me what I needed to know.

Director: And what did you need to know?

Scientist: That I could do it on my own.

Director: But if you go with a mentor all the way, isn't that where he or she leaves you? On your own?

Scientist: Mentors never truly leave you on your own. They always want a part of them to be there, too.

Director: But isn't it just common decency to let that part be there?

Scientist: Not if it gets in your way.

Backers (Friend)

Friend: Sure, if you have a big enough destiny you need backers, investors in your destiny. And they must get paid.

Director: Why would anyone want to invest in someone else's destiny?

Friend: Like I said, they want to get paid. And if you think your destiny is big, you have to think about this fact.

Director: But if you think too much about it, might it not interfere with your destiny? Do you know what I mean?

Friend: Of course I do. The distraction caused by dwelling on this can undermine your cause.

Director: So maybe you need a middle man. Someone who manages the backers in order to leave you free to focus on your destiny.

Friend: Yes, that might be what you need. But there's a danger there, too.

Director: What danger?

Friend: That the middle man promises too much.

Director: I see. But what if it only seems to be too much?

Friend: How so?

Director: He or she sees more of your worth than you yourself see.

Friend: Meaning you're inclined to sell yourself short?

Director: Yes.

Friend: Then the middle man plays a valuable role.

Director: Agreed. But what happens when you learn just how much has been pledged?

Friend: There might be a problem.

Director: Why?

Friend: Because if the promises are big they might cause you to lose your nerve. Which means you won't achieve your destiny. And that would be more than a shame.

Wrongs (Artist)

Artist: Don't let wrongs done to you take you from your destiny. All too many do.

Director: How would a wrong take you from your destiny?

Artist: Oh, it might sap your confidence or make you waste your whole life lusting for revenge. Things like that.

Director: So what must you do?

Artist: Overcome the wrong.

Director: How?

Artist: By digesting it.

Director: Digesting it? What does that mean?

Artist: It means you allow the wrong to nourish you.

Director: You mean you learn from it? But what do you learn?

Artist: How to strike out boldly and act for destiny rather than merely to react to wrong.

Director: But can't we strike out boldly and act for revenge?

Artist: Almost all revenge is mere reaction.

Director: Then tell me. What's the boldest thing we can do?

Artist: As far as wrongs go? Put them into perspective.

Director: But aren't there wrongs so great you can never do that?

Artist: Not as many as people like to believe.

Director: You do know what people will say to that, don't you?

Artist: Of course I do. They'll say I never suffered much wrong.

Director: Have you suffered much wrong?

Artist: I've suffered things that aren't obvious. And so I'd be a fool to say I'm a victim of great wrong. But all the little things add up. Yet I refuse to let them dominate my life.

CREATIVITY (SCIENTIST)

Scientist: We all have our breaking point. Those with great destinies flirt with theirs all of their lives.

Director: Breaking point? Are you talking about having a mental breakdown, Scientist?

Scientist: Yes.

Director: But why flirt with something like that? Wouldn't you want to steer clear at all costs?

Scientist: Some costs are too great to pay.

Director: How can that be? What's more important than staying sane?

Scientist: If it's your destiny to be creative, truly creative — whether in science, or art, or leadership, or whatever — you have to push the limits. Sanity, as we all know, is essentially about respecting these limits. If you go a little too far and don't respect where you should — that's it. But you have to take the chance.

Director: But why? What do you get out of being creative?

Scientist: How can you even ask that? Creativity is an end in itself.

Director: Hmm, I wonder. When you push the limits, is it possible you'll end up creating a new limit? A limit that people will respect?

Scientist: Yes, of course.

Director: Then isn't that an end of creativity?

Scientist: The limit or the respect?

Director: Both. And there's more than one kind of respect. They'll respect you for having created that limit they respect. Isn't that true?

Scientist: I suppose it is.

Director: So, to be sure, creativity, in addition to being an end in itself, establishes new limits, and generates twofold respect.

Scientist: Yes, but your motives must be pure. To you, creativity must simply be an end in itself. If not, you put too much pressure on yourself. And that can drive you mad.

JUDGMENT (FRIEND)

Friend: Following your destiny is a constant exercise of judgment.

Director: You mean you don't just get set in your way and that's that?

Friend: No, of course not. You're always evaluating where you are and where you're going and what you need to do.

Director: Is that all you evaluate?

Friend: What do you mean?

Director: Don't you have to evaluate others?

Friend: Of course. That's just as important as evaluating yourself.

Director: So what does it take to judge others well?

Friend: You have to know what to do with them.

Director: Like keep them close or push them away?

Friend: Exactly.

Director: Is there anything more important in living your destiny than who you keep close or push away?

Friend: Nothing. I'm even tempted to say that almost all of destiny is just that.

Director: Have you ever had to push someone you cared about away?

Friend: I have, a friend. There was just no other way.

Director: Why?

Friend: Because he was interfering with my life.

Director: So you judged your 'life' to be more important than friendship?

Friend: Yes.

Director: Hmm. And you were sure there was no other way to stop the interference?

Friend: I was — because the interference was the basis of our being friends.

DRIVEN (ARTIST)

Artist: A character of destiny is without interest unless driven by that destiny.

Director: A character in a play, for instance, yes. But what about in real life?

Artist: It's the same, as far as I'm concerned.

Director: What does it mean to be driven?

Artist: The opposite of what it means to drive.

Director: We can drive our destiny?

Artist: At times we can, yes.

Director: Steadily, and gently, and right on track?

Artist: Yes, yes. Boring, isn't it?

Director: But what a magnificent thing!

Artist: Magnificent and boring, true.

Director: You prefer something that verges on the wild and out of control?

Artist: Along with the rest of the human race, I do.

Director: But you and the rest of the human race only enjoy these things vicariously?

Artist: As if that surprises you. Most people don't want to be driven to the edge of sanity. But they enjoy watching others who are.

Director: And if one day destiny sneaks up on them and starts to drive?

Artist: They'd better tell it to stop in no uncertain terms.

Director: You think it would listen?

Artist: Destiny can only drive the complicit.

Director: But you know that's not all there is to it.

Artist: And tell me why that is.

Director: Because the moment you tell destiny no, you're forced to deal with fate.

Dreams (Scientist)

Scientist: How do dreams relate to destiny? Dreams are what we have when we're asleep. Destiny is what we have when we're awake.

Director: So should we try to align the two as closely as possible?

Scientist: Well, I'm not aware of any proven technique to control your dream life. So are you asking if we should believe in our dreams and model our waking life on them?

Director: Yes.

Scientist: Of course we shouldn't. It's madness to try such a thing.

Director: But there are people who believe in signs from dreams, you know.

Scientist: I know all too well. My mother believed in dream signs.

Director: Really? Did she do anything about them?

Scientist: Did she? Director, she kept me home days from school because of her bad dreams.

Director: Did she ever have good dreams?

Scientist: Oh, sure. And then she was manic.

Director: It's funny, though.

Scientist: How so?

Director: We don't always remember all of our dreams. That means a significant part of our dream life is unaccounted for.

Scientist: It is funny. You might have a sign from a good dream right before you have a bad dream. But the bad dream wakes you up. And so you forget the good and remember the bad.

Director: So it's foolish to rely on signs from dreams without remembering them all. And even if we could remember them all.... But what about destiny, the dream we have when we're awake?

Scientist: Will it give us signs? Yes. And we can remember them all. Or at least we should. And when we do, we trust they'll lead us someplace good.

UNITY (FRIEND)

Friend: A person of strong destiny can unify others. That's true even while these others pursue their own independent destinies away from this person, all on their own.

Director: Independent unity? How does that work?

Friend: It works.... You.... You do... the same things on your own!

Director: The same things on your own? What things?

Friend: You serve the cause.

Director: The cause?

Friend: I can't explain.

Director: That's okay. But who is this strong person of destiny?

Friend: It's 'person of strong destiny', not 'strong person of destiny'.

Director: Sorry. Who is this person?

Friend: It's — you!

Director: Me? I'm not aware of having such a strong destiny.

Friend: But of course you are! And your friends know it, too.

Director: Know that we're unified even when we're apart?

Friend: Yes. You encouraged them to go off and live their independent lives.

Director: How did I do that?

Friend: By living your own.

Director: So finding my own way encouraged them to find their own way away from me? But, Friend, whatever unity you think there is aside, it seems to me you mean I always lose my friends!

Friend: No. Despite or because of their absence you have the strongest possible bond.

Director: Hmm. But if all of this is true — then why are you still here?

Friend: It's simple. I've yet to find my way.

FUTURE (ARTIST)

Artist: Who do you think makes the future?

Director: You mean the death and birth of stars and the like?

Artist: Of course not. I'm talking about the human future.

Director: Who makes that? Why, don't we all?

Artist: Yes, yes. But some of us more than others. No?

Director: You mean some people are destined to have a great influence over others, and that influence shapes the future?

Artist: Just so. And that influence can be bad or good. Yes?

Director: Naturally.

Artist: So tell me, Director. What does good influence bring?

Director: A good future.

Artist: And what does bad influence bring?

Director: A bad future.

Artist: Very good. But now answer this. With what idea is a good future tied up?

Director: The idea of progress.

Artist: Yes. So what do we want those who are destined to shape the future to do?

Director: Make progress.

Artist: Right again. But you know it's not that simple.

Director: I can think of several ways in which it's not that simple. But let me tell you one. There's 'progress', and then there's progress.

Artist: Perfectly so. And do you know what people should fear? That the force of this distinction won't be felt where it's needed most.

Director: Where will it be needed most, my excellent friend?

Artist: Between the two of us I have no doubt we can make an educated guess.

Quiet Life (Scientist)

Scientist: Can you have a destiny if you have a quiet life? Of course! There's much you can do in quiet that can't be done in noise.

Director: Like what?

Scientist: Well, you can think.

Director: Why does thinking take quiet?

Scientist: You have to be able to hear yourself.

Director: And when you hear yourself what happens?

Scientist: You find your way to destiny.

Director: Destiny is a sort of inner voice?

Scientist: Yes, I think it is.

Director: But you know what they say about people who hear voices....

Scientist: Yes, but note — they talk about 'voices', not a single voice.

Director: And destiny always speaks to you in a single voice?

Scientist: Yes.

Director: But what if you're forced to leave your quiet life and enter the noisy fray?

Scientist: You take what you learned from your inner voice with you.

Director: But what happens as circumstances change?

Scientist: What do you mean?

Director: I mean doesn't your inner voice give a running commentary on changing things, a commentary you can't hear when you're in the noise?

Scientist: I think that's true.

Director: So if you have to live in noise, what must you do?

Scientist: Come back to quiet as often as you can.

Mind (Friend)

Friend: All good destinies require you to have a mind of your own.

Director: I agree. And would you take it further?

Friend: In what way?

Director: This. Does having a mind of your own mean you necessarily have a good destiny?

Friend: I'm not sure.

Director: Why not?

Friend: Because can't villains have minds of their own?

Director: I suppose that's true. But we wouldn't say they have good destinies.

Friend: No, of course not.

Director: So what does it mean to have a mind of your own, a good mind of your own, one that gives you a good destiny?

Friend: It means you're independent.

Director: What does that mean?

Friend: It means you decide based on what you think, not on what others tell you to think.

Director: Hmm. I wonder.

Friend: Wonder what?

Director: I wonder if that doesn't define in a backhanded way what a villain is.

Friend: How so?

Director: A villain tells you what to think and then expects that you'll obey.

Friend: Yes, of course. And a hero expounds a point of view and then leaves it to you to decide.

Director: Then let's be heroes to each other, Friend — and drive the villains away.

GAIN (ARTIST)

Artist: Anyone who walks with destiny hopes to gain. Some hope for love. Some hope for power. Some hope for fame. You can't find anyone who has a destiny who doesn't hope to get something out of it.

Director: What if someone just hopes to go out for a nice little walk?

Artist: A nice little walk with destiny? Ha! It doesn't work like that. Destiny is a disruptive force.

Director: And we gain by the disruption it causes?

Artist: Yes. The disruption creates possibilities.

Director: Possibilities for love, or power, or fame?

Artist: Yes, yes — and sometimes all three.

Director: I can see people wanting these things. But who really wants disruption itself?

Artist: I'll tell you. People who are bored.

Director: We walk with destiny because we're bored?

Artist: There's no greater gain than finding something interesting to do. Wouldn't you agree?

Director: I suppose there's some truth in that. So let me see if I understand. Destiny is disruptive. Disruptions create possibilities. And possibilities allow us to do interesting things.

Artist: Yes. So it only follows that we stand to gain from destiny every time.

Director: So long as the 'interesting things' we gain don't overwhelm us.

Artist: Well, of course — but that's the chance we take.

Director: Is that why you don't take the chance? For fear of being overwhelmed?

Artist: In a sense. You see, I'm always almost overwhelmed by my art. A destiny would only serve to put me over the edge. Besides, my art itself disrupts. In fact, I'd say that destiny and my work both serve the very same end — possibilities and interesting things.

Director: Then art excuses lack of destiny — if this bold assessment of your work is true.

Proving (Scientist)

Scientist: The greatest mistake someone can make is to hope to use their destiny to prove something to others.

Director: I'm not sure I understand. Can you say more?

Scientist: Of course. Destiny only proves itself. It's no use trying to prove something about someone else's destiny by means of your own.

Director: I'm still not sure I understand. Are you saying that if someone with a remarkable destiny says to everyone: You can do it, too! Just look at me! — that's the height of foolishness?

Scientist: Precisely.

Director: Why do you think that is?

Scientist: As I said, your destiny can only prove the truth of your destiny — yours alone.

Director: And no two destinies are alike?

Scientist: Absolutely not. That's why it's so sad to see people trying to copy the destiny of others. It can never be.

Director: Then what good is looking to the destiny of another?

Scientist: There's only one possible good. And that's if you learn that you must focus solely on yourself, on your own destiny — to the exclusion of everything else.

Director: So you don't look to those of your scientific peers who you take to be destined to do great things?

Scientist: I look to their work, to their technique — and I learn from them. But as far as their destinies themselves? I don't give them a second thought.

Director: What would happen if you did?

Scientist: I'd be wasting my time. Or worse.

Director: What 'worse'?

Scientist: I'd prove to others, others who know — that I'm not worthy of the destiny I claim.

Opposition (Friend)

Friend: No destiny worth having comes unopposed.

Director: Why do you think that is?

Friend: It's partly psychological. If nothing opposes you, you'll probably think what you're doing isn't worth doing.

Director: Opposition confers a sense of worth?

Friend: Yes, I think that's true.

Director: Hmm. I wonder if you'd create your own opposition when nothing else opposes you.

Friend: You mean mentally? I bet you would. Haven't you heard people say you can be your own worst enemy?

Director: I have. But tell me. Aside from yourself, what's the greatest opposition you can have?

Friend: That of a great and true enemy.

Director: You mean someone who wants to destroy you no matter the cost?

Friend: Yes.

Director: Even at the cost of their own destiny?

Friend: Director, an enemy like this would see destroying me as their destiny.

Director: And maybe it would be. But I think we need to go back to the notion of opposition conferring worth.

Friend: Why? You don't think it's true?

Director: No, I don't. I think we certainly need to overcome opposition at times. And doing so can be sweet. But sweetness isn't worth. Or is it?

Friend: No, sweetness isn't worth. Worth is worth.

Director: Then let worth confer worth, and don't confuse worth with anything else. And, Friend, don't miss out on something worthwhile — simply because nothing stands in your way.

TRAINING (ARTIST)

Artist: Just as you would train yourself in an art you must train yourself in your destiny.

Director: So how do you train yourself in an art?

Artist: First you study the works of others.

Director: So you train yourself in your destiny by first studying the destinies of others? What's next?

Artist: You study some more.

Director: And then?

Artist: You forget almost everything you learned.

Director: And what are you left with?

Artist: Mostly? Yourself.

Director: And is knowledge of yourself enough for destiny and art?

Artist: Assuming you've learned something about others along the way? Yes.

Director: You surprise me, Artist. Why only 'something' about others?

Artist: Let me guess. You're asking yourself, What else is art about if not judging people for what they are?

Director: I was asking that.

Artist: And you should ask it for destiny, too. I mean you can't stay on your path if you can't judge others properly. They'll knock you off your way.

Director: You're reading my mind.

Artist: Well, here's the trouble. Things can get confused.

Director: In what way?

Artist: We learn about others while learning about ourselves. The problem is, we might mix the two up. It happens more often than you'd think. So we should remember only 'something' — the key thing — about others, but everything about ourselves. Then we're prepared. But don't ask me what the 'key thing' is. You need to figure it out yourself.

PERSECUTION (SCIENTIST)

Scientist: The early scientists were persecuted. And their destiny was all the greater for it.

Director: Are you suggesting that persecution can amplify destiny?

Scientist: If you hold fast in the face of it? Yes.

Director: What made early scientists the object of persecution?

Scientist: Their methods and discoveries threatened people's beliefs.

Director: Do people always persecute those who threaten their beliefs?

Scientist: Always.

Director: But surely it can't be 'always'.

Scientist: Why not?

Director: If it were 'always' how would science have progressed?

Scientist: Well, yes — of course. I should say, there will always be some who actively persecute others for threatening their beliefs.

Director: Just as there will always be those who simply go along passively with the persecution?

Scientist: Yes.

Director: But there will always be some who support the persecuted. No?

Scientist: True. But it's often too few, too late.

Director: Too late for what?

Scientist: For preventing the persecution of being burned at the stake!

Director: Literally so?

Scientist: In some ages, yes.

Director: But in other ages?

Scientist: There are other means.

SELLING YOUR SOUL (FRIEND)

Friend: What does it mean to sell your soul?

Director: To abandon your destiny.

Friend: But what does it mean to abandon your destiny?

Director: To give up on who you are.

Friend: But if you are who you are, how can you give up on yourself?

Director: You might not be who you are.

Friend: But now this sounds like nonsense. How can you not be who you are?

Director: You can be who you are on your own, and someone else with others.

Friend: Ah, that's a good point. I think that happens to a lot of people. But what do you think about people who are afraid to be by themselves?

Director: You mean they go rushing out to others at every chance, as if they were trying to avoid themselves?

Friend: Yes, exactly that.

Director: Well, I think they're selling their souls.

Friend: But are you suggesting you have to be alone to keep your soul?

Director: No, but it's a bad sign if you're afraid to be alone, especially if for a short while.

Friend: I agree. Now, suppose you've sold your soul. How can you get it back?

Director: It's simple. You take up your destiny once more.

Friend: Once more? You assume we've all taken it up?

Director: Most of us at one time or another have, usually when we were quite young. But then many of us put it back down.

Friend: But your destiny is always there, waiting for you to take it back up?

Director: Yes, and isn't that the reason why so many people are afraid to be alone? They can't stand the sight of that destiny staring them full in the face.

STAY TRUE (ARTIST)

Artist: Here's a good three act play for you. Character finds destiny. Character abandons destiny. Character wins destiny back.

Director: You make it sound so simple.

Artist: It is.

Director: Then why haven't you written it?

Artist: How do you know I haven't? Maybe I'm planning a posthumous publication.

Director: That's not your style.

Artist: What's my style?

Director: Getting what you can, while you can.

Artist: Ha! So what if it is?

Director: I have no problem with that. With a style like that, you're likely to stay true.

Artist: True to myself? But why?

Director: Because you always want more.

Artist: Alright. But what about you? What's your style?

Director: To find characters who are living in act two of your play.

Artist: And usher them into act three?

Director: It's not that simple, my friend. They must prepare themselves to win their destiny back before they enter act three.

Artist: So you appear in the middle act, the turning point of the play, and help them to prepare?

Director: That's my style — right there in the thick of things.

Artist: The thick of things before the real fight! But what if the characters beg, positively beg you to help them win destiny back when they struggle for their life in act three?

Director: I stay true and remain in act two. I'm of no use in someone else's act three.

RANK (SCIENTIST)

Scientist: I would rather hold the humblest of ranks and stay true to my destiny than hold the highest and stray off of my way.

Director: Nobly spoken.

Scientist: Thank you. But it's true. And I think it's true for you, too. Isn't it?

Director: I follow my path wherever it goes. Or maybe I should say I cut my path wherever I'd go.

Scientist: Yes, I like that better.

Director: And if high rank is what I want, high rank is what I'll have.

Scientist: I believe it.

Director: But there comes a point where that's no longer true.

Scientist: What do you mean?

Director: There comes a point when you've cut a path and followed it so far that holding high rank may no longer be possible. You might be too far away. But this is also true in another sense.

Scientist: What other sense?

Director: When you've followed a path so long and so far, far away from high rank and all that comes with it — it may no longer be possible to want high rank.

Scientist: Wanting high rank is no longer possible? You know, there are those who would say you're not speaking truth.

Director: Why would they say that?

Scientist: Because they think that when you get so far away you realize that what you truly want is rank. But now it's no longer possible to have it. And so you lie about what you want.

Director: But what profit is there to lie?

Scientist: You can save that thing so closely related to rank. You can save face.

Director: But who will see that face so far out along my way?

THE PRICE (FRIEND)

Friend: Yes, some people find the price of their destiny to be too high. But I think they've forgotten.

Director: Forgotten what?

Friend: That it's never as high as the highest price in the world.

Director: Which is?

Friend: Regret.

Director: So you should be willing to pay any price for your destiny?

Friend: Yes, any price.

Director: But, Friend, this doesn't sound like you.

Friend: What do you mean?

Director: You're usually a bit more... conservative.

Friend: Conservatives can't have destiny?

Director: Of course they can. But when you speak of paying any price....

Friend: I know. But you agree with me, don't you?

Director: Well, I do. I, too, would pay any price — except the price of regret.

Friend: Then you'd never deny me the same.

Director: How could I? But tell me. How do you know you're not paying too much?

Friend: What do you mean? The price is the price.

Director: You think the price of destiny is fixed? Oh, but that isn't always true! We must bargain for destiny's sake. Or at least we should.

Friend: Why?

Director: Because you need to get as much destiny as you can for whatever you've got. Otherwise, you'll feel you sold yourself short. And can you think of any greater reason for regret?

Monsters (Artist)

Artist: Some people view people of destiny as monsters.

Director: And how do people of destiny view these people who view them so?

Artist: As less than what they could be.

Director: What makes the destined seem to be monsters?

Artist: To these people? The better question is — what doesn't?

Director: Well, what doesn't?

Artist: Nothing! Assuming, of course, the destined are living up to their potential.

Director: What is that potential?

Artist: Full humanity.

Director: But, Artist, are you saying that poor you, with no destiny, can't live up to that?

Artist: Ha! I'm beyond all that.

Director: You're superhuman, yes?

Artist: I'll take the question as a compliment. And what are you?

Director: Me? I like to think I'm as human as they come.

Artist: Then you know great destiny is yours?

Director: I'm not presumptuous enough to say. But even if I have a modest destiny, I could do with out the monstrousness.

Artist: Then you'll have to get off your way and court the ones who see you as a monster of destiny. And that, my friend, is hardly to your taste. Or have I got you wrong?

Director: There's really no way out?

Artist: Well, you could go... my way.

Director: And what exactly is your way?

Artist: Oh, but you know! Supporting destiny without having it yourself. But I know, I know — in certain ways that's the most monstrous thing of all!

Shooting Stars (Scientist)

Scientist: No, I wouldn't care to be a shooting star. Though I do believe there are those who are destined to be precisely that.

Director: But do you think shooting stars want to be what they are? Do they want to burn brightly for a short while and then disappear?

Scientist: I think there are those who would do anything to burn brightly, no matter for how long.

Director: But it's better to burn brightly for a long while, isn't it?

Scientist: It's best to simply be a star, a fixture in the sky, shining on and on.

Director: And yet shooting stars move a great many people, no?

Scientist: True.

Director: Why do you think that is?

Scientist: Shooting stars often seem, and sometimes are, brilliant. And when they're gone, the sense of loss is great.

Director: Well, what can we tell these shooting stars? Look, we'll say, if you can only hold out for a while and save up your strength — just stop giving it all away — you'll have a chance at being a star fixed in the heavens!

Scientist: Yes, but do they really have that chance? Isn't the lack of that chance precisely what makes them burn the way they do?

Director: You may have a point.

Scientist: And there's more. They don't want our offer of a spot in the heavens.

Director: Why?

Scientist: Because they know full well the people they've moved will fix a place for them in a heaven of their own.

Director: So there are two types of heaven? One that gives off starlight. And another that gives off... what?

Scientist: Gives off the light of all those memories that still burn bright.

Rising Star (Friend)

Friend: When we're with our destiny, we always feel like we're a rising star.

Director: Even at the height of our career?

Friend: Always rising, yes.

Director: Then destiny is a very powerful force.

Friend: Of course. Did you have any doubt?

Director: Well, yes. I didn't know it was as strong as that. I mean when we're at the height of our career, who knew that we can still rise? Speaking strictly, of course.

Friend: Strictly speaking? You feel you're at your height — but you're not.

Director: Ah, I see. Destiny ignores the illusions we might have about our maximum height.

Friend: Yes, I think that puts it well.

Director: And so you rise.

Friend: And you take your place in the sky.

Director: And yet still you rise.

Friend: Beyond the sky?

Director: Where else? You rise, and rise, until you inhabit the icy cold regions of furthest off space.

Friend: I'm not sure that's where you want to be.

Director: Why not?

Friend: You might be too far away to be seen from Earth.

Director: But what does it matter so long as you keep rising, my friend?

Friend: It matters to me.

Director: Being seen means that much?

Friend: It does. Because in the end, if no one can see you — then what's the point?

Setting Sun (Artist)

Artist: There's one thing to remember, Director. When the Sun sets it doesn't know it's setting.

Director: That sounds profound.

Artist: What it sounds like is truth.

Director: Oh, I don't know, Artist. Couldn't the Sun see the Earth turning and know that to the Earth it's both rising and setting at once all the time?

Artist: Yes, yes. But if so, do you wonder if it ever feels sad?

Director: Whether the Sun feels sad for the Earth as it sets?

Artist: Yes, leaving us all alone in the dark.

Director: But we're not all alone. We have the Moon and the stars.

Artist: The Moon? Ha! A feeble reflector of light.

Director: Well, what about the stars, cousins to our Sun? Aren't they good company in the night?

Artist: Yes, I suppose you have a point. But they're too far off to have any real destiny that links with our own — for now.

Director: Only the Sun is close enough for that?

Artist: Only the Sun.

Director: And if another star approached?

Artist: But stars don't approach. They all have their fixed place in the sky.

Director: But if one did?

Artist: One left its place and came toward us? We'd be destroyed.

Director: But what if the Sun somehow drove it away?

Artist: The Sun would have to leave its place to fight the star — and that, Director, would be the end.

Rebirth (Scientist)

Scientist: Sometimes it takes being reborn to reach our destiny. And that means we need to be prepared to die, so to speak.

Director: When must we be reborn?

Scientist: When the way we're on is bad.

Director: And are we often on a way that's bad?

Scientist: Very often, yes.

Director: So people are dying and being born again all the time?

Scientist: No, Director. It's rare that people die and come back to life.

Director: But why?

Scientist: Most just keep on their bad way until the end of their lives.

Director: But why would they do that if they can be reborn?

Scientist: I think they're afraid.

Director: Afraid of rebirth?

Scientist: Afraid of the death that precedes rebirth.

Director: They're afraid they'll die and won't come back?

Scientist: Precisely. So this takes faith — the greatest faith there is.

Director: And when they take that leap, when they're reborn — what do they come back as?

Scientist: What else? As those who live their proper way.

Director: But what about the ones who don't have to die?

Scientist: You mean they live their destiny right from the start?

Director: Yes. Surely they don't need rebirth.

Scientist: That may be. But I think that's much more rare than you might think.

Repetition (Friend)

Friend: While it's true that living your destiny never gets boring, that doesn't mean we don't have to repeat ourselves often.

Director: Well, good things bear repeating.

Friend: Yes, that's so true.

Director: Why do you think we have to repeat ourselves?

Friend: One, to remind ourselves of what's important. Two, so people know what to expect of us.

Director: I understand the first point. But what do you mean by the second?

Friend: When people get used to us living our destiny they tend to offer us less resistance.

Director: They take it for granted in us?

Friend: Yes, exactly. And so they don't complain.

Director: Why would living our destiny be grounds for complaint?

Friend: The complainers aren't living their own, and when they see us living ours, it reminds them of that fact.

Director: But if we keep on repeating things pertaining to our destiny in front of them, will they ever really get used to it?

Friend: More so than if we merely mention our destiny now and then. In that case, each mention seems like a fresh injury. But if we talk about it all the time, they get sick of it and ignore us.

Director: Is that our strategy, then, my friend? To make people sick of us so they ignore us?

Friend: Better that than to have them up in arms against us all the time.

Director: But why not say nothing to them, and repeat ourselves often only among friends?

Friend: Because silence is always more hated than speech.

COMFORT (ARTIST)

Artist: The destined can take comfort in their destiny. But it's the comfort of a hard camp bed.

Director: Comfort is comfort. But why do you insist that comfort be hard?

Artist: Because destiny is hard and it's only fitting that the comfort it brings be hard, too.

Director: What's hard about destiny?

Artist: Ha! If you don't know that by now, I can't help you.

Director: Really, Artist — what's hard about destiny?

Artist: If you're really living your destiny you feel like you always want to give up.

Director: But I don't believe that for a minute! Sure, I believe there are times when you want to give up. But to feel like that all the time? That's ridiculous. I think you get this notion from the characters you create. You make them excessively dramatic that way.

Artist: Excessively dramatic? I make them real, given the circumstances they operate in!

Director: So it's the circumstances that make them want to give up? Not something essential to destiny?

Artist: Yes, yes. The circumstances are hard. That makes for more drama, as you say.

Director: But you can live your destiny without hard circumstances, can't you?

Artist: I suppose. But if living destiny is comfortable, then what's the point?

Director: What's the point if living destiny is hard? It's really the same question. What's the point of living your destiny?

Artist: Honestly? I don't know.

Director: And yet your characters have destinies.

Artist: Yes, and they figure out the point themselves.

Director: Can they be comfortable before they've figured it out?

Artist: Of course not. It's anguish for them not to know what their destinies mean. And so the dramatic tension builds and builds — until it's clear.

Pleasure (Scientist)

Scientist: All good destinies involve pleasure, whether it's the pleasure of learning a new fact or of winning a great victory.

Director: Do bad destinies involve pain?

Scientist: Yes.

Director: Is that how you know whether your destiny is good or bad? You judge by the pleasure or pain you feel?

Scientist: Well, I'm not sure I'd like to say that.

Director: Why not?

Scientist: Because you can have a good destiny and go through a period in your life in which you feel much pain. Your destiny still is good.

Director: But how do you know that at the time? I mean you don't know when the pain will end. Might you not start to think you have a bad destiny?

Scientist: True.

Director: So you should never assume you have a bad destiny. You should always try to find pleasure in life and feel your destiny is good. Do you agree?

Scientist: I agree.

Director: But let me ask you this. Do you think it's possible to feel pleasure and pain at once?

Scientist: I'm not so sure about that.

Director: Well, what if you're a fighter and you win a close match? You might be in great physical pain, but you feel great pleasure at having won. Possible?

Scientist: I suppose.

Director: And can't it be that way with all of our destinies? Struggle and pain, victory and pleasure?

Scientist: True enough.

Director: Then let's tell the ones in pain that it gets better when they win.

Joy (Friend)

Friend: Any destiny devoid of joy isn't a destiny worth living.

Director: How does joy differ from pleasure?

Friend: Joy is a heightened sort of pleasure.

Director: A sublime pleasure?

Friend: Yes.

Director: So even if you have a great deal of pleasure in living your destiny, it's not enough unless there's joy?

Friend: That's my belief.

Director: What if you have a great deal of pain in living your destiny — and yet you have some small amount of joy?

Friend: Well, that's the hard question. Would I want a life like that over a pleasant life devoid of joy? I think I would.

Director: What if you only experienced joy once in your life, and the rest was pain?

Friend: I still would choose that life. But I have to say, you're posing the extreme case.

Director: There are many more joys to be had in life?

Friend: A great many. Simple joys.

Director: But aren't simple joys dangerously close to simple pleasures?

Friend: Well, you might have a point.

Director: How do we distinguish the two?

Friend: Joys stir you deeply. Pleasures don't.

Director: Pleasure is more superficial?

Friend: Yes, I think that puts it well.

Director: So the choice is between the deep and the superficial life?

Friend: Yes. And as far as I'm concerned, there is no choice to make.

The End (Artist)

Artist: Anticlimax is common among the destined.

Director: What do you mean?

Artist: The end comes and there's no great big bang. The end just comes.

Director: You mean the destined just fade away?

Artist: They can. And sometimes they just drop dead on the spot.

Director: But, Artist, when you speak of anticlimax, are you speaking from the perspective of the destined themselves, or from that of their loved ones?

Artist: From the perspective of the loved ones, of course. They're the ones who expect something great. But from the perspective of the destined? They simply feel they're coming home to peace.

Director: But really, Artist, what do those who feel let down expect? A deathbed pronouncement?

Artist: Yes. They hope the destined will reveal at long last their secret, their truth.

Director: But there is no secret to destiny. Is there?

Artist: You're asking me? Well, I'll tell you what my own deathbed scene might be. If I'm so 'lucky' as to fade away, I'll pretend I have a secret truth. I'll string everyone along.

Director: Until?

Artist: Until I see the one who looks me in the eye and smiles a knowing smile. And then I'll go, as happy as can be.

Director: You want your lie called out.

Artist: Of course I do — in service of the truth!

Director: And, in the end, is that what all your art has served?

Artist: The truth? Well.... You see.... It's not so easy to say.

Director: Then will you at least admit your art served truth better than you?

Artist: Ha! I will.

ENDS (SCIENTIST)

Scientist: Do the ends of destiny always justify the means?

Director: Justify them to whom?

Scientist: Ah, that's an excellent question. Justify them to you, the one of destiny.

Director: No, I don't think they always do. In fact, I think it might be the other way around.

Scientist: The means justify the ends?

Director: Why not?

Scientist: Yes, but what if we love the means but don't want the ends? Don't you think that's possible?

Director: I do. But if we employ the means they're going to draw us closer to the ends. And when we can see the ends what do you think we'll find?

Scientist: That the means and ends are of a piece?

Director: Yes. And then the chance seems good we'll learn to love the ends.

Scientist: So we just employ the means with no clear ends in view?

Director: Doesn't that happen every day? We simply do what we love.

Scientist: But what if we never find our ends?

Director: Then doing what we love is an end in itself.

Scientist: I don't know. I mean, that's not really an end. And it just seems sort of... shallow.

Director: Means and ends should always be deep?

Scientist: Maybe 'deep' isn't the right word. How about 'meaningful'?

Director: I can agree to that.

Scientist: Good. But if we don't know the end, how can we be sure of its meaning?

Director: I guess we can't. And it might be for others who come after us to decide.

BEGINNING (FRIEND)

Friend: Each fulfilled destiny causes a seed to sprout in someone else's soul.

Director: That's rather poetic, Friend.

Friend: Thank you. Do you think it's true?

Director: Is it that the fulfilled destiny serves as inspiration?

Friend: Yes.

Director: Then yes, I think it's true.

Friend: And do you know what this brings?

Director: Tell me.

Friend: A sort of immortality.

Director: From full growth to seed, to sprout, and so on, and so on eternally?

Friend: Yes.

Director: But what guarantee is there that the cycle will go on?

Friend: Well, that's the thing. There is no guarantee.

Director: Really? It's not the inevitability of nature's way?

Friend: There's nothing inevitable when it comes to human things.

Director: Hmm.

Friend: What are you thinking?

Director: I'm thinking that means so much is at stake.

Friend: Everything is at stake.

Director: That's a lot of pressure on people of destiny, no?

Friend: True, but they're used to pressure from simply living their lives.

Director: Then there's no need to train them for greater affairs?

Friend: No, there isn't. They're part of the greater in just being themselves.

Printed in the United States
By Bookmasters